SHARKS

DESIGNED BY PHILIP CLUCAS
EDITED BY BARRY VARNEY
PRODUCTION: RUTH ARTHUR, DAVID PROFFIT, SALLY CONNOLLY
DIRECTOR OF PUBLISHING: DAVID GIBBON
DIRECTOR OF PRODUCTION: GERALD HUGHES

For Gonzalo

Grateful thanks to Professor Sam H. Gruber for his invaluable comments on the text.

CLB 2356
All photographs drawn from the files of Planet Earth Pictures Ltd.,
This 1995 edition published by Tiger Books International PLC, Twickenham
© 1990 Colour Library Books Ltd., Godalming, Surrey
Printed and bound in Spain by Gráficas Estella, S.A. Navarra.
All rights reserved
ISBN 1-85501-394-0

SHARKS

TERESA FARINO

**TIGER BOOKS INTERNATIONAL
LONDON**

For many people the word "shark" conjures up a picture of a vicious, man-eating fish, armed with a fearsome array of teeth and of dimensions akin to that of a Greyhound bus; an image which has undoubtedly been reinforced by the film industry of recent years. The truth of the matter is that, of approximately 370 species so far discovered, only a fraction conform to the "Jaws" stereotype. Most sharks are a far cry from this voracious predator – the nightmare of bathers the world over – and are harmless creatures, displaying a great variety of form, lifestyle and feeding habits.

Eight orders of living sharks are currently recognized, distinguished on the basis of such physical characteristics as the presence or absence of an anal fin, the number of gill slits and dorsal fins, the position of the mouth and the possession or otherwise of a nictitating membrane, or third eyelid. The most primitive order is considered to be the Hexanchiformes, easily identified by their six or seven gill slits as compared to the normal complement of five. This small order contains only five species, including the eel-like frilled shark, which derives its name from the wavy posterior margin of each gill slit. The Squaliformes, or dogfish sharks, number over 80 species in three families. The bramble sharks (Echinorhinidae) are characterized by a few, greatly enlarged denticles scattered over the body, while the humpbacked or angular sharks (Oxynotidae), such as the humantin, have a high, triangular body in cross-section. The main family, however, is the Squalidae, to which belong the only species to be found in polar waters (the Greenland shark), the smallest species (the dwarf lanternshark) and the most abundant species (the spiny dogfish).

The five members of the Pristiophoriformes are unmistakable, each having an extended, sawlike rostrum. They are thus known collectively as sawsharks, not to be confused with the similar sawfish, which is a type of ray. The Squatiniformes, or angelsharks, is another small order comprising a single genus in which all 13 members are markedly flattened dorsoventrally and superficially resemble rays. The eight species which make up the Heterodontiformes, the bullhead or horn sharks, are among the most easily recognized of all sharks, with their blunt heads and characteristic ridges over the eyes. They are unusual among sharks in having both biting and crushing teeth, from which the Latin name of the single genus, *Heterodontus* – literally "different teeth" – is derived.

The Orectolobiformes is a rather mixed bag, although all species have a pair of barbels on the underside of the snout and two dorsal fins. Here is included the largest living fish, the whale shark, along with such strikingly marked bottom-dwellers as carpet sharks, wobbegongs and bamboosharks. The blind shark, so called because it closes its eyes when out of the water, and the more typically sharklike nurse sharks, also belong to this order.

Similarly, the Lamniformes is probably not an irrefutable classificatory unit, made up of seven families containing only 16 species. The current members of this group range from the herculean basking shark of the ocean surface to the bizarre, deep-sea goblin shark, from threshers, with their whiplike upper tail lobes to the recently discovered plankton-feeding megamouth shark, and from the most feared of all sharks, the great white, or maneater, to the ferocious-looking but relatively placid sand tigers.

The last order is that of the Carcharhiniformes, or ground sharks, which is also the largest, containing over 200 species in eight families. Around half of these belong to the Scyliorhinidae, known as catsharks in the United States and dogfish in Great Britain; a family which includes the aptly-named swellsharks, which wedge themselves into rocky crevices to avoid predation by swallowing large quantities of sea water. Another large family, the Triakidae, contains the houndsharks and smoothhounds. The Carcharhinidae, or requiem sharks, currently number 49 species of what might be termed "typical" sharks, many of which are so similar that even experts have difficulty telling them apart. Most are highly predatory sharks, including such well-known species as lemon, blue, tiger and bull sharks. The eight species of the Sphyrnidae are very similar to the requiem sharks in most physical aspects except that their heads are flattened and extended laterally, with the eyes, and usually the nostrils, situated at the extremities. Not surprisingly these sharks are known as hammerheads.

Sharklike fishes have been in existence for almost 400 million years. Although shark teeth have been found in early Devonian deposits, the earliest complete skeleton discovered was that of *Cladoselache*, dating from around 350 million years ago. Even at this primitive stage, the resemblance to modern-day sharks was striking.

By the close of the Cretaceous, some 63 million years ago, it is thought that shark evolution was more or less complete, with most modern shark families in existence. Although this was the time of widespread extinctions, when the great dinosaurs of land, sea and air mysteriously vanished forever, sharks somehow weathered the crisis, and appear to have changed very little in the process. This lack of alteration in basic shark design over millions of years suggests that sharks were able to make the necessary physiological and behavioural adjustments to environmental variations without the modifications in basic morphology that usually accompany such changes.

The most famous of all extinct sharks is undoubtedly *Carcharodon megalodon*, which is now thought to have disappeared as recently as 11,000 years ago. This vanished giant is known only from its teeth, which are remarkably similar to those of the great white except that they measure an incredible 4.7 inches from base to tip and about 6 inches across at the widest point. Early estimates of the size of this beast suggested a length of over 98 feet and a weight of more than 50 tons, although these dimensions are now thought to be greatly exaggerated; a maximum length of around 42.5 feet is now believed to be more reasonable.

Some living sharks are so close to ancient forms that they are known as "living fossils." The frilled shark, which has jaws very similar to that of *Cladoselache*, is the sole living representative of an extinct species, known only from fossil teeth, which is thought to have lived some twelve to twenty million years ago. It is unique among sharks in possessing an undivided cartilaginous notochord, rather than well-defined vertebrae, and a lateral line system which consists of little more than open grooves in the sides of the fish.

There are two main types of fish in the world today. The Osteichthyes, or so-called "bony" fish, make up some 97 percent of all species, the remainder belonging to the Chondrichthyes – the cartilaginous fish – which comprises sharks, skates, rays and chimaeras. The main physical difference between these groups is that bony fish, as their name suggests, have a skeleton composed of bone, whereas in sharks and their relatives the skeleton is composed of cartilage.

Cartilage is a flexible skeletal tissue formed from groups of rounded cells lying in a matrix containing collagen fibres. In bony fish and higher vertebrates it is invaded and replaced by bone cells, or osteocytes, at an early stage of development to form true bone. But although shark cartilage may be reinforced with small interlocking plates of apatite (an extremely hard substance composed largely of calcium phosphate) at points of stress, such as the skull, jaws and vertebrae, sharks and other members of the Chondrichthyes are entirely boneless.

Cartilage decays rapidly, thus complete skeletons of early sharks are rare in the fossil record. On the other hand, shark teeth, which are composed almost entirely of apatite, decompose very slowly. They are so abundant in marine deposits that much of our knowledge of ancient sharks is derived solely from their study. Although it was once believed that the presence of a cartilaginous skeleton was a primitive feature in an evolutionary sense, the absence of shark teeth in the fossil record until about 350 million years ago, well after the majority of bony fish had appeared, suggests that the shark skeleton may represent a pseudoprimitive condition, having reverted to a cartilaginous state.

On the whole, bony fish have a rather hit and miss method of reproduction. Huge numbers of eggs are produced (in some species, tens of millions), fertilization is usually external and few survive to adulthood. Sharks, on the other hand, produce relatively few offspring – litters of over a hundred are extremely rare – but these are released from the female in such an advanced state of development that almost all survive birth, although figures for lemon sharks suggest that up to 50 percent succumb to predators within the first year of life. In some species, the young sharks are even nourished within the uterus by a form of placenta similar to that seen in mammalian reproduction.

Most bony fish have an air-filled swim bladder which considerably increases their buoyancy. The absence of this organ in sharks is to some extent compensated for by a lighter skeleton and by their large, oily livers (oil being lighter than water). In some sharks the liver may account for over a quarter of the total body weight, but even so they are still heavier than water, and obliged to swim continually if they are to maintain their position in the water column. However, sand tigers, which swim very slowly, and sometimes even hang motionless in the water, have been observed rising to the surface and gulping air into the stomach; a habit which no doubt aids this species to maintain its customary position.

While bony fish have a protective rib-cage around the viscera, this is never present in sharks, although some short ribs may extend from the vertebral column. A further difference is that sharks have a remarkably short intestine, containing a unique structure known as the spiral valve. Rather similar to a spiral staircase in configuration, it greatly increases the surface area, and thus the absorptive capacity, of the gut without the need for long loops of intestine which would reduce the amount of visceral space available for the liver. The gill arrangement in the two groups is also very different. Sharks possess between five and seven external apertures, known as gill slits, whilst these structures are shielded by a flat operculum, with a single, posterior opening, in bony fish.

The body of a bony fish is protected by a series of overlapping scales which increase in size as the fish grows. Sharks, on the other hand, are covered with small, toothlike structures called dermal denticles which are continually shed and replaced with slightly larger models as the shark matures. A further distinction is that shark teeth are not set firmly in the jaws as are those of bony fish, but are located instead in the gums. Like the dermal denticles, from which they are in fact derived, the teeth of a shark are continually shed and replaced throughout its life.

In bony fish the two lobes of the tail are generally more of less equal in size, whereas in sharks the vertebral column extends into the upper lobe of the tail, which as a result is better developed than the lower lobe in most species. In some bottom dwelling sharks the lower tail lobe may be almost nonexistent, the upper lobe lying almost parallel with the body; such fish are obliged to swim in an eel-like manner. Exceptions to the asymmetrical, or heterocercal, design are the fast-swimming sharks of the open ocean, in which the two lobes may be almost equal, and the angelsharks, the only order in which the lower tail lobe is longer than the upper.

A typical shark of the open sea has a streamlined outline. The snout is more or less pointed, the body slightly flattened, the fins triangular and the tail large and upturned. As such it is one of the most graceful fish in the sea, swimming with sinuous movements of the body. Because sharks have no swim bladder they must keep moving if they are not to sink slowly to the bottom. Propulsion is provided by the tail, but its asymmetrical nature means that the nose of the shark is pushed downwards in the process. Compensatory lift is provided by the flattened underside of the snout and by the broad pectoral fins, but in order to fulfil this function, the pectorals have become rigid, rather like the wings of an aeroplane.

This is in marked contrast to the highly mobile fins of bony fish, which can be manipulated in almost any direction, allowing their owner to hang motionless in the water, stop suddenly and even swim backwards. Sharks, however, rely heavily on their highly supple vertebral column and powerful tail to avoid obstacles. A shark moving at high speed can brake abruptly by using its pectorals as flaps and curving its body into an S-shape to stop dead.

Although it has long been thought that sharks are coldblooded creatures, it is now known that several species are in fact able to maintain their body temperatures above that of the surrounding water. Most, if not all, of the Lamnidae, or mackerel sharks – including makos, porbeagles and great whites – as well as the threshers of the family Alopiidae, are now known to possess a type of heat exchanger known as the rete mirabile: literally "miraculous net." It consists of a dense network of capillaries in the muscle blocks which surround the vertebral column, which absorbs heat from blood returning to the gills. In some species, such as the big-eye thresher, the rete mirabile is also found below the eye. These sharks are thus able to retain a greater proportion of their metabolic heat than other fish and when active have body temperatures 12-20°F higher than their environment, so increasing the rate of muscle contraction. The main benefit is to assist both swimming speed and efficiency, and it is surely no coincidence that the mackerel sharks are among the fastest and most agile in the world, also renowned for their ability to leap spectacularly out of the water.

Although studies on the speeds at which sharks swim in the open ocean are extremely difficult to carry out, blue sharks have been calculated to attain speeds of around 40 miles per hour in short bursts. Makos, which are probably the fastest fish in the world, have been recorded at velocities of over 59 miles per hour. Normally, however, even the most rapid of pelagic sharks cruise at an energy-saving pace until the opportunity to feed arises.

Sharks obtain oxygen by passing water in through the mouth, over a fine surface network of capillaries in the gill arches, then out through the gill slits which are located on the sides of the head. It was once believed that sharks had to swim constantly in order to keep this current of water flowing: to stop was to drown. Typical bottom-dwelling species, however, have an opening behind the eye which connects directly to the throat known as the spiracle. Through the spiracle, which is in fact a modification of the first gill slit of ancient fishes, a steady flow of oxygenated water can be passed over the gills; a fact which enables species such as carpet sharks and wobbegongs to lie in ambush, and also prevents the gills from becoming clogged with mud or sand, which would certainly be the case if these bottom-dwelling sharks were to draw in water through the mouth.

Recently, however, more active species such as nurse, lemon and bull sharks have been observed motionless on the sea floor, opening and closing their mouths in order to pump water over the gills. There have also been recent discoveries of other fast-swimming shark species apparently "sleeping" on the sea bed, although this appears to occur only under certain conditions. This behaviour has been observed in whitetip reef sharks and banded houndsharks in the Indopacific as well as in Caribbean reef sharks, although the best documented example is that of tiger sharks near Mexico, "sleeping" in highly oxygenated waters subjected to incoming fresh water. It is considered possible that the high oxygen content may allow the sharks to breathe without swimming, although another theory is that the excess oxygen and low salinity have a narcotic effect on the sharks.

Obtaining data on the maximum size of the world's various shark species has been likened to chasing the Loch Ness monster, since fishermen are legendary exaggerators of the dimensions of the "one that got away." Even dead specimens were rarely measured accurately until recent times; the literature is littered with overestimations of shark size and weight. It is now known that sharks, unlike most vertebrates, never quite stop growing, although once they have reached sexual maturity the increase is much less noticeable. A recently proposed theory is that maximum size is determined by the amount of visceral space available for the liver, since the larger the shark, the greater the proportion of the body cavity that must be dedicated to this organ in order to give the same degree of buoyancy.

The largest of all sharks, and indeed of all fish, is the aptly named whale shark, which has been reliably measured at something over 39 feet, possibly reaching a gargantuan 59 feet. The weight of such a beast is in the region of 13 tons. The basking shark is also of monumental proportions, possibly attaining 49 feet in length, although on verifiable records it does not exceed 32 feet. It is perhaps fortunate that both these species are harmless plankton-feeders, although accidents in which boats have been capsized have been recorded.

The largest of the predatory sharks is generally considered to be the great white; exaggerations about the length of this fearsome species are legion. There is a rather dubious record of a 29.5-foot specimen caught off the Azores in the mid-Atlantic, now revised down to between 19.5 and 23 feet, but the largest reliable records are around 23 feet, such as that caught near Malta in the Mediterranean Sea in April 1987. Vying with the great white for the title of largest predator is the tiger shark, which frequently exceeds 19 feet in length, while the great hammerhead commonly attains 16 feet. Other large sharks are the Greenland shark at 21 feet and the megamouth shark at 15 feet, while great hammerheads and sixgill sharks may approach 19.5 feet in length.

Taking the group as a whole, more than half of all sharks are less than 3 feet long, about 80 percent never exceed 2.5 feet and only 10 percent grow to more than 9 feet in length. To date, the smallest shark known to man is a deep-water species called the dwarf lanternshark, in which mature females measure some 7-8 inches and the males only 6-7 inches.

The maximum age to which a shark may live is, if anything, even more difficult to ascertain than its maximum length. It has been suggested that great whites may live for almost a century with similar estimates given for the spiny dogfish. Studies indicate that the school shark, or tope, has a maximum lifespan of some 50 years, similar to that of lemon sharks, while the colossal whale shark is thought to live for more than 60 years. Owing to the late stage at which sharks reach sexual maturity – at an incredible 15 to 20 years in the spiny dogfish, for example – these estimates are not unreasonable if a species is to have any chance of maintaining itself. Average shark longevity, however, is estimated at less than 25 years.

Sharks are found in all the world's oceans, from the tropics to the subpolar seas, while some species are even born in and spend their entire lives in fresh water. Some sharks are predominantly coastal in their distribution, whilst others are truly pelagic, found only in the open sea. Some frequent surface waters, others are confined to the sea bed and some of the most bizarre species live at depths where the light of the sun never penetrates.

A few sharks are almost cosmopolitan in their distribution, ranging through all the world's oceans. The blue shark is possibly the most widespread of all sharks, ranging from north of Norway to southern Australia, although it tends to stick to waters between 59° and 70°F, while the mako is also found in temperate and subtropical waters almost worldwide.

On the whole, however, most species display distinct preferences as to their habitat, usually dependent upon the depth or the temperature of the water. Very warm water, for example, in excess of 89°F, is generally avoided since it contains less oxygen than cool water and makes life difficult for active sharks, although lemon sharks have been found to tolerate temperatures of up to 140°F. Whale sharks are more or less confined to tropical seas and the great hammerhead is seldom found in waters of less than 75°F. The oceanic whitetip, which has been described as probably the most abundant large animal on the face of the earth (large being defined as weighing more than 99 pounds), occurs wherever waters are more than 70°F and over 656 feet deep.

By contrast, the only shark to enter Arctic waters is the Greenland sleeper shark, which is even known to venture beneath the polar ice cap. The porbeagle seems to select waters of 64°F or cooler while sixgills and sevengills also prefer cold water; in tropical regions they occur mainly in deep water, whilst in the polar regions they occupy shallower zones.

The spiny dogfish is found in all temperate and subpolar waters, avoiding waters cooler than 41°F and warmer than 59°F, from the coastal shallows to depths of around 656 feet. It is not, however, found in the tropics, and it is interesting to speculate as to how such a bitemperate distribution arose. It is thought possible that these small sharks were able to cross the equator at a time when the earth's tropical belt was much narrower than it is today. Although there are at present no marked differences in the northern and southern hemisphere populations, prolonged geographical isolation should eventually lead to the evolution of separate species.

Pelagic sharks are remarkably uniform in color, with a lightish underside and a dark dorsal surface, which may range from brown, through purple, to blue, often with a metallic sheen. Such coloration is known as countershading; the white belly blends in with the sunlit surface of the sea when viewed from below, and the darker back is difficult to make out against the darker color of deep waters when seen from above. Countershading thus affords the shark a degree of concealment even in the open ocean, which may be vital in a surprise attack on its prey.

Some sharks are known only from deep waters, and as such they must be tolerant of very cold water temperatures. The deep-water catshark, for example, is known to live at depths of more than 5,577 feet in the northwest Atlantic, the eel-like false catshark occurs as deep as 4,921 feet and a Portuguese shark has been retrieved from a trap set at 8921 feet. Cookiecutters have been recorded from depths of more than 11,483 feet in tropical and subtropical waters and it is highly probable that sharks as yet unknown to man exist in even deeper waters.

Various physical characteristics distinguish these deep-water sharks. They are often dark in colour – sometimes almost black – with very little countershading. Large eyes which are extremely sensitive to low light levels are another feature of abyssal sharks, seen in species such as the blackbelly lanternshark, also known as the devil shark. Poorly calcified skeletons, loose skins and flabby bodies are also typical of deep-sea sharks, as a result of the lack of available minerals and the huge pressure exerted by several miles of water overhead.

Many deep-water sharks are bioluminescent; that is, they possess organs known as photophores, containing either light-emitting organic compounds or symbiotic bacteria which themselves possess compounds that emit light. The pygmy shark, found at depths of up to 4,921 feet, has many ventral photophores which emit light only while the fish is moving, possibly enabling it to escape detection whilst at rest. The cookiecutter is one of the most brilliantly luminous of all sharks and the green lanternshark also has an elaborate and distinctive pattern of photophores.

The exact function of bioluminescence in marine organisms is still only speculated upon, although suggestions include protection from predators below them by means of counter-illumination, location of the opposite sex in an almost lightless environment and the attraction of prey.

Just as some sharks are found only in the ocean abyss, yet others occur only in shallow waters around the coastlines and coral reefs of the world. The majority of these shallow-water species are benthic, or bottom-dwelling by custom, the most extreme examples being the angelsharks. With their winglike pectoral fins and flattened bodies angelsharks spend most of their lives resting on the sea bed waiting for unwary fish to come within range. In order to assist the ambush, angelsharks are well camouflaged, with gray-brown spotted skins and often half bury themselves in the sand. Although generally considered lethargic, they can lunge quickly to trap their prey, their jaws being structured to shoot out rapidly, forming a large, toothed tube.

Wobbegongs have modified skeletons in their pectoral fins which permit them to "walk" on the sea bed. They often crawl in preference to swimming and the spotted wobbegong has even been observed clambering from one rock pool to another above the surface of the water. Many wobbegongs and carpetsharks are patterned with brilliant colors so as to blend in with the rocky or coral bottom and may even have "weedy" fringes of flesh around the mouth to help disguise them further, or to lure prospective victims within reach. Hornsharks, too, possess cryptic coloration, with bold stripes breaking up the outline so as to make them almost invisible whilst motionless on the sea bed.

Some of the more sharklike sharks to frequent shallow water include the sand tiger, which commonly occurs in waters between 6 and 33 feet deep. Nurse sharks are also predominantly inshore fish, often resting on the sea bed in waters so shallow that their dorsal fins protrude from the surface, while tiger sharks, among the most predatory of all species, are not infrequently encountered in waters so shallow that they can hardly swim, although they are equally at home in the pelagic zone.

Most sharks are restricted to the saline waters of the oceans but the bull shark commonly enters fresh water. This species has been found more than 500 miles from the ocean in Africa's Zambezi river and over 1,863 miles from the mouth of the Amazon. The sharks which occur in Lake Nicaragua in Central America are now also known to be bull sharks, although for many years they were considered to be a separate, freshwater species. Despite numerous rapids in the Río San Juan, which links this lake to the Caribbean Sea, bull sharks manage to migrate upstream and so into the lake. Sharks which have spent some time in the lake have brownish undersides more in keeping with its often cloudy waters, whilst recent arrivals still bear the characteristic white bellies of ocean-going bull sharks.

Following the initial description of the various freshwater sharks as different species, scientific opinion then converted to the view that these were almost certainly all bull sharks. However, a recent reversal of this theory has occurred with respect to the Ganges shark. It is now thought probable that both bull sharks and a distinct and little known species – the Ganges shark – occur in this Indian river. These are the only two shark species known to regularly enter fresh water, although it is still not known how long they spend there or, perhaps more importantly, how they manage to overcome the physiological problems associated with a conversion from marine to fresh water habitats.

In the tropics, where the water stays at more or less the same temperature all year round, sharks may remain within a fairly limited area for most of their lives. In more variable conditions, however, such as those experienced in temperate regions, bottom-dwelling species may be provoked to move into deeper water during the cold season. Nurse sharks and other shallow water species simply become less active with a drop in water temperature, but most of the requiem sharks regularly undertake long migrations in response to seasonal changes. It is thought that such migrations are sometimes brought about largely by changes in the water temperature, and thus the availability of food, but more importantly, for the purpose of reproduction, as is discussed later.

Shark tagging studies are the source of most information on the migration patterns of pelagic sharks. It has been found, for example, that blue sharks commonly travel over distances between 1242 and 1863 miles, the record for this species being almost 3726 miles from New York State to Brazil. Makos, tiger sharks and sandbar sharks have all been known to travel over 1,552 miles; one mako shark tagged off New York was recovered off Senegal (West Africa) eighteen months later, having undergone a transatlantic journey of at least 3576 miles.

The basking shark is found in all temperate to subarctic waters, excluding the Baltic Sea, sometimes travelling in schools numbering hundreds of individuals. In the North Sea, the regular disappearance of this enormous shark at the onset of winter long puzzled scientists, but it is now thought that they spend the cold months "hibernating" on the sea bed, probably due to the paucity of the plankton on which it feeds at this time of year. It is thought that the basking shark utilizes this rest period to shed and regrow its gill rakers in preparation for the next year's plankton harvest. In the warmer waters off California, however, the basking shark is able to feed all year round. The presence of large numbers in Californian waters during the European winter has led to recent speculation that some basking sharks may migrate across the Atlantic rather than hibernating.

For many people the word "shark" is synonymous with a mental picture of row upon row of gleaming, razor-sharp teeth. Although some species, especially the more active predators, do have teeth which fit this description, there is in fact such great variation in the form and function of shark teeth that a species can often be identified from its teeth alone.

Slender teeth, such as those of the sand tigers and goblin sharks, are usually associated with fish- or squid-eating species, since a good grasp is essential to prevent such slippery prey from escaping. Short, small teeth in many rows form a rough pavement in members of the family Triakidae such as the leopard shark, for holding and crushing marine invertebrates – molluscs, sea urchins and crustaceans. The teeth of the great plankton-feeding sharks are tiny and vestigial, those of the basking shark being only about one twelfth of an inch long.

In some species the teeth are markedly different in the upper and lower jaws. The lower teeth of the kitefin shark, for example, are broad-based with a sharply serrated triangular blade, whilst those in the upper jaw are lanceolate and point inwards. The sixgills and sevengills of the family Hexanchidae have broad, slanting lower teeth, each possessing many parallel points, or cusps, like tiny combs; they are completely unlike those of other living sharks.

In the birdbeak dogfish of the genus *Daenia*, not only are upper and lower teeth different, but variations are present between the sexes as well. In other species juvenile teeth vary from those of the adults, making accurate identification difficult.

The horn sharks of the genus *Heterodontus* have both crushing and biting teeth, but instead of being located in different jaws, the biting teeth are found at the front of the mouth, while the rear teeth take the form of grinding plates. The four species of humpback sharks of the Oxynotidae have a very strange arrangement of upper teeth. There are usually six rows of functional teeth, the first row being composed of only two or three teeth, but each successive row containing a greater number, thus forming a roughly triangular patch on the roof of the mouth. Very little is known about the biology of these strange sharks, and the exact function of this dental structure is as yet unrevealed.

It is thought that the maximum number of teeth which a shark may possess is around 3,000 (although many have considerably fewer), arranged in six to twenty rows; only the first couple of rows are in use at any one time. The remainder, the replacement teeth, are in various stages of formation. They lie in a vertical whorl within the gum, the points facing backwards, and are erected for use as required. It has been estimated that a typical predatory shark may get through more than 20,000 teeth in an average lifetime.

Many sharks, including great whites and hammerheads, lose their teeth a few at a time, although other species, such as the cookiecutters, lose a whole set at a time. The cookiecutter also has the largest teeth in proportion to its size (a maximum of 16.5 inches) of any shark. A further curious feature of the cookiecutters and other deep-sea fish is that they frequently swallow these shed teeth, the evidence having been found in the stomachs of captured specimens. It is thought that this may guard against the loss of valuable calcium and phosphate in the ocean depths, where such minerals are present only in very small amounts.

Various feeding strategies, both in terms of preferred prey and methods of feeding, exist within the group, but without exception all sharks are carnivorous. Although some, such as the tiger shark, may occasionally scavenge, there are no "vultures" among this group of fish.

Three of the largest species of shark are plankton feeders – the whale shark, the basking shark, and the recently discovered megamouth shark – although the techniques by which they extract these microscopic organisms from the sea are very different.

The basking shark has very long gill slits which almost join up beneath and above the head. Internally each gill arch possesses between 1,000 and 1,300 gill rakers, resembling long, flexible bristles, which are derived from the dermal denticles. When the mouth is open these gill rakers are pulled erect, forming a coarse sieve which strains the plankton from water passing in through the mouth and out through the gill slits. The gill rakers have mucus-secreting glands at the base which effectively ensnare the plankton. When the mouth is closed the gill rakers return to their former position, flat against the gill arch and the mucus-plankton mixture is squeezed into the mouth and thence into the stomach. In order to feed most efficiently the basking shark cruises, mouth agape, at around 1.25 to 2.5 miles per hour. A 23-foot individual has been estimated to filter some 52,972 cubic feet of water per hour.

In the whale shark, by contrast, each gill arch is connected to its neighbor by numerous lateral bars of cartilage supporting masses of spongy, finely meshed tissue through which the water is forced, leaving the plankton behind. Whale sharks have also been observed amid schools of tuna which themselves are feeding on large shoals of small fish or squid. The sharks position themselves vertically in the water, heads at the surface, and repeatedly lower their mouths to just below the surface so that tons of water, containing both tuna and the bait fish, rush into their gullets.

The way in which the megamouth shark feeds is still a mystery, since only three specimens of this bulky deep-sea giant have ever come to light; the first in 1976 off Hawaii, the second in Californian waters in 1984, while a third was reputedly washed up on a western Australian beach in 1988. The latter specimen was around 13 feet long, with a mouth some 31 inches across. It is presumed that megamouth, so called for its enormous gape, feeds on plankton and other small creatures because its teeth, like those of the former two species, are minute. Its lower jaw and tongue are very dark in colour, but the inside of the upper part of the jaws is lined with a curious tissue which may have bioluminescent properties. One theory is that megamouth swims with its mouth wide open and small marine organisms are attracted to the silvery light.

Bioluminescence is also thought to play a large part in the way in which other deep-sea sharks feed. The green lanternshark lives at depths of between 1148 and 1312 feet in the Gulf of Mexico. Although it grows to a maximum of around 9 inches in length, the eyes and horny beaks of much larger cephalopods have been found in its stomach. A recent suggestion is that this species may hunt in packs, the individual sharks recognizing one another, and thus maintaining the integrity of the school in the darkness, by the unique pattern of photophores. In this way green lanternsharks are able to tackle much larger prey than would be the case if they were to hunt singly. A similar theory has been proposed for the devil shark, or blackbelly lanternshark, a slightly larger relative of this species.

Many fish and invertebrates of average size spend their days in the ocean depths, rising to the surface each night to take advantage of the rich plankton broth under the cover of darkness. Although this strategy is designed to minimize predation, there are nonetheless several shark species that have adopted the same timetable in order to feed on these medium-sized marine organisms. The 10-inch pygmy shark, for example, follows the diurnal vertical migration of its prey, rising to the surface at dusk and descending, replete, to the depths at dawn, probably undertaking a round trip of some 1.25 miles in the process. The 9-foot night shark, unusually for a member of the Carcharhinidae, also resides in the ocean depths by day, migrating to the surface at night to feed.

While some bottom-dwelling species of shallow waters, such as horn sharks and zebra sharks, have strong, flattened teeth in the rear of the mouth with which to grind up their preferred diet of sea urchins and molluscs, other benthic sharks have different methods of feeding. The sawshark, for example, in addition to flailing at passing fish with its long, serrated snout, also uses this appendage for stirring up the bottom sediments to dislodge burrowing organisms. Some biologists consider that the elongated rostrum of the deep-sea goblin shark may serve a similar function.

Sharks of the family Carcharhinidae either swallow their intended prey – usually large fish – whole, or remove chunks of flesh with their serrated teeth. The jaws and teeth of such a shark are more than equal to this task, the maximum force exerted having been measured at something in excess of 3 tons per square centimetre. As the shark approaches its intended victim, the snout is raised and the lower jaw is projected downwards and outwards, thus substantially increasing the gape. Since the jaws are unable to move substantially in a horizontal plane, the shark flails its body from side to side to augment the scissor-like motion required to remove a mouthful.

The mature great white shark feeds on large bony fish such as tuna, sea turtles, other sharks and rays and even marine mammals, especially seals, although the young of this voracious species are less ambitious in their dietary habits, selecting smaller fish, crustaceans and other marine invertebrates. The bull shark, on the other hand, appears to have a predilection for the young of other shark species, especially its close relative the sandbar shark. Most of the large pelagic sharks prefer living prey, although they will sometimes take carrion; tiger sharks especially have a reputation for scavenging.

Thresher sharks, in which the upper lobe of the tail may account for almost half the total length, have a bizarre technique for catching their prey. The elongated tail-fin is incredibly flexible and there are reports of it being used with great accuracy by the thresher to stun individual fish at the surface of the water, and even for throwing the unfortunate victim straight into its mouth. It has also been suggested that the tail may be used to herd small fish into a tight shoal before feeding, so avoiding energy expenditure in pursuing individuals; most of the threshers caught on long lines are hooked in the tail!

The cookiecutter shark has a fascinating method of feeding on marine creatures which are substantially larger than itself, especially swordfish, but also marlin, tuna, dolphins, elephant seals and large whales. Although itself a feeble swimmer the cookiecutter lies in wait for its victims in the open sea. Should a potential meal pass by, this diminutive shark attaches itself by means of its fleshy lips, creating a vacuum with its powerful tongue. The cookiecutter then rotates its body like a top, possibly assisted by the current of water flowing past its moving and probably oblivious target, scooping out an almost perfectly hemispherical chunk of flesh with its two sets of razor-sharp teeth. These circular wounds in the bodies of whales and large fish long puzzled scientists, but their origin has now been satisfactorily explained.

In an environment where suitable prey might be infrequently encountered, many sharks are able to survive for long periods without feeding, drawing on the huge reserve of fat in the liver in the meantime. In addition, several species are known to be able to hold food in the stomach for days without commencing the digestive process, although how this happens is uncertain. Sharks are also able to regurgitate undesirable objects by everting their stomachs through their mouths.

How do sharks locate their food? Although sharks have always been renowned for their keen sense of smell, it has long been thought that their other senses were dull in the extreme. But recent research has proved this to be far from true; sharks are in fact among the most perceptive of all living creatures.

The nostrils of a shark are not involved in breathing, but are discrete organs located on the front of the head. Water which enters the nostril as the shark swims is directed into the nasal capsule where it passes over a series of sensory lamellae before leaving via a second aperture. These olfactory lamellae are situated very close to the large and highly developed olfactory lobe of the forebrain, thus minimizing the time interval between the stimulus and its detection by the shark. Experiments have shown that sharks are able to detect one part of human blood in 10 million parts of sea water; this olfactory sensitivity is thought to be enhanced even further in starving individuals.

When a shark scents something interesting in the water it will automatically turn towards the source; that is, in the direction of the prevailing current. As each nostril alternately receives the stronger stimulus, the shark describes a sinuous course along the scent trail. It is thought that the greater the distance between the nostrils, the more efficiently the shark is able to pinpoint the source; hammerheads, with their nostrils at the extremities of "hammer," are thought to be especially adept in this respect.

All sharks possess paired inner ears which are connected to the outside world by tiny ducts. Resembling the inner ears of most vertebrates, each is composed of two large sacs, the sacculus and the utriculus, off which open three semicircular canals. These three canals lie on different planes: two vertical and at right angles to each other, the third horizontal. At the base of each canal lies a swelling called the ampulla, housing sense organs that respond to the direction of gravity, thus allowing the shark to maintain its upright position in the water. Sound, which is detected as particle displacement, is picked up by sensory organs in the sacculus which contain hair cells. Different shark species are sensitive to different ranges of such "sounds," the most predatory species probably having the widest range. Lemon sharks, for example, respond to vibrations between 100 and 1,500 Hertz, which is about equivalent to the mid-range of human hearing.

Similar cells to those in the sacculus are found in the lateral line system, which consists of subcutaneous canals filled with a gelatinous fluid running along each side of the shark's body and branching around the head. These sensory receptors are able to pick up particle displacement caused by the movements of other creatures, or those created by the shark itself as it approaches a stationary object. The lateral line system has been described as the shark's sense of "distant touch."

Sound travels farther and faster in water than on land; sharks are attracted to irregular, low frequency vibrations, particularly those of less than 40 Hertz at distances of up to about 330 feet. There is speculation that these low frequency waves, typical of the vibrations produced by a wounded fish, are picked up by the lateral line, whereas higher frequencies are detected by the acoustic system.

Although sharks have long been regarded as creatures with poor sight, research carried out between 1960 and 1975 has proved that this is not the case. A shark's eye is not unlike that of higher vertebrates, including man, although the lens is rather more rigid. Most sharks have both rods and cones in the retina, which theoretically means that they should be able to detect differences in color; they have been shown to be particularly sensitive to contrasts between light and dark. The most predatory sharks, such as carcharhinids and threshers, are thought to excel in the detection of moving objects, even in dim light. The lemon shark, for example, although very far-sighted, has been shown to possess a slightly greater sensitivity to light than man.

Perhaps the most interesting feature of the shark's eye is the tapetum lucidum, consisting of a series of silvery plates located behind the retina. In dim conditions, light which has already passed through the eye is reflected back by this mirror-like layer, thus increasing the sensitivity of the retina. In bright light, however, in order to protect the retina from overexposure, a layer of pigmented cells called melanoblasts spreads over the plates of the tapetum lucidum, thus reducing the reflection. Some deep-sea sharks, because they live in perpetual twilight, lack these melanic "sunglasses" and the tapetum lucidum is exposed at all times. This is detected as a luminous greenish shine in the eyes of such creatures when they are hauled to the surface, similar to that seen in the eyes of a cat caught in car headlights.

Owing to prominent eye muscles, sharks are able to maintain an almost panoramic visual field, even when twisting and turning. Some species have fixed eyelids, in some sharks they are mobile, while four families also have a third eyelid, or nictitating membrane. In all cases these function as physical shields, to protect the eyes from damage rather than to control the amount of light entering.

In addition to a keen sense of smell, good auditory perception and reasonable eyesight, sharks have also been recently proved to have a higher sensitivity to electrical stimuli than any other animal ever studied. In a classic set of experiments, small spotted catsharks were shown to be capable of detecting an electric field as low as 0.01 microvolts percentimetre: more than 25 million times weaker than the faintest that man can perceive, and less even than the electrical charge produced by the nerves of a living organism.

Electroreception, as this ability has been called, is probably accomplished by isolated sensory cells known as the ampullae of Lorenzini, which are located on the underside of the shark's snout, although the exact manner in which they function has yet to be ascertained. This acute sensitivity to electric fields is extremely useful to the shark in detecting prey at close range. Sharks have been shown unerringly to locate flounders buried beneath the sand. On the other hand, divers in shark cages attest to the fact that a shark initially attracted to flesh bait will often mistakenly bite at the cage rather than the bait at the last minute, possibly because of the strong galvanic current or corrosion current – a type of electrical field – produced by the metal in sea water.

Some researchers (Gruber and Kalmijn) have recently demonstrated that sharks are even able to utilize their electroreceptive abilities to detect the weak electric fields generated by the ocean currents flowing through the earth's magnetic field, using such information to orient themselves in the open sea, for navigation and for migration over long distances.

Members of the Orectiolobiformes, most sawsharks and some false catsharks have barbels at the front of the head which may be used to "taste" the sea bed in search of suitable quarry, although some workers maintain that these are purely tactile organs. In addition, most sharks have taste buds on the floor of the mouth, the tongue and the pharynx, which are used as a final test as to the edibility or otherwise of their prey.

To locate suitable prey, therefore, sharks are equipped with a more than adequate array of senses. In a typical predatory shark, olfactory and auditory stimuli, which may be detected at a range of hundreds of yards, are thought to provoke exploratory behaviour. A shark following a scent trail or low frequency vibrations will eventually come within visual range of its quarry, although even in the clearest water it seems that about 65 feet is the maximum distance.

It seems that certain movements, such as those produced by a wounded fish, in addition to the strong olfactory and auditory signals which it is now receiving, will stimulate the shark to attack. As the shark closes on its victim, the eyes either roll back in the sockets, as in the case of the great white, or the nictitating membrane covers the eye, as in the requiem sharks, to protect it from any possible damage during the encounter. The shark is now attacking blind, and it is thought that the ampullae of Lorenzini are responsible for guiding it during these crucial last moments. The ultimate test is that of taste; an unpalatable object may be bitten, but is often rejected.

A long-reported characteristic of many observations on shark feeding habits is that of the so-called feeding frenzy. This occurs where many sharks are attracted to the same prey, and possibly as the result of sensory "overload." Some workers suggest feeding frenzies are caused by the powerful vibrations produced by the head-shaking actions of the first shark to feed; others maintain that the stimulus is largely olfactory, provoked by a sudden increase of the concentration of blood in the water. What is certain is that the frenzy does not commence until the prey has been attacked at least once.

Shark senses are not only used in detecting prey and navigation, but are in all probability also employed in finding a mate, for the all-important process of reproduction.

Among some species of shark, especially the carcharhinids, there is a marked tendency for sexually mature individuals to segregate by sex. Males and females are rarely seen in the same area except during the mating season. In some species, especially those with a formidable jaw armature, it is thought that the males develop an inhibition to feeding at the onset of the mating season, possibly to protect the females from any cannibalistic tendencies. Once courtship and copulation have been accomplished, the sexes again separate and the males resume feeding.

Gravid females are also believed to stop feeding as the time of birth approaches, again to avoid the temptation of cannibalism. In many carcharhinid sharks the birth takes place in specific nursery grounds, usually in warm, shallow waters, which must be outside the normal geographical range or preferred habitat of the sexually mature males of the species. The females remain only long enough to give birth and resume feeding after their departure.

Male sharks are easily distinguished from female sharks, even at a glance, by the presence of trailing appendages known as claspers in the region of the pelvic fins. Claspers are elaborate structures with their own complicated muscles, skeleton and innervation, the inner edges of which have rolled up and overlapped to form a groove or tube. The structure is very variable, being more or less flattened or cylindrical, smooth or covered with denticles to act as holdfasts during copulation, according to the species.

Female sharks have two ovaries which are located close to the mouths of a pair of oviducts, although they are not directly connected. Even if only one ovary is functional, therefore, which is the case in a number of shark species, both oviducts are able to receive eggs.

Sharks also display what are known as secondary sexual differences, that is, those which are not directly connected with reproduction. In many species, the female is markedly larger than the male; male bigeye houndsharks, for example, are on average only two-thirds the length of the female and may weigh only one-sixth as much. In the African spotted catshark, however, the male is considerably larger than the female, while male porbeagles average 8.5 feet and females only 7 feet, although this is a rare phenomenon.

Male sharks often have much longer teeth than females of the same species in order to grasp her more firmly during courtship. This is seen in dogfish of the genus *Daenia*, in which the teeth of the males are much more erect, while mature male narrowmouth and redspotted catsharks have longer teeth with fewer cusps than the females. Such sexual dimorphism with respect to dentition is also seen in the barbeled houndshark and the bigeye thresher, although perhaps the most extreme example is that of the broadgill catshark, in which the teeth of the male are more than twice the length and take the form of a single conical cusp, as opposed to the short, three-to five-cusped teeth of the female.

In species which display these dental variations between sexes, the skin of the female is generally much thicker in the region where the male may grasp her during courtship; female blue sharks, for example, have hides up to twice as thick as those of the male, a phenomenon also seen in the barbeled houndshark.

Owing to the difficulties associated with studying shark behaviour in the wild, our knowledge of their courtship and copulation is extremely patchy. In smallspotted catsharks which have been observed mating in captivity, the slender-bodied male is able to wind himself completely around the female, which remains immobile in the normal swimming position. The larger sharks, however, are unable to copulate in this way, since their bodies are far less flexible, a side-by-side approach having been observed in nurse, sand tiger and bamboo sharks.

Fertilization is internal in all sharks, the male inserting first one clasper, then the other, into the cloaca and oviducts of the female. A seawater pump system flushes sperm into the female's cloaca.

Some sharks exhibit delayed fertilization. The female blue shark, for example, can store sperm for months after insemination, waiting for the eggs to mature before fertilization takes place. In other species, such as the basking shark, the spermatozoa are moulded into thin-coated packets known as spermatophores before insertion into the female. As such they are more easily stored by the female shark, the thin coating dissolved only when the sperm are needed to fertilize the eggs.

Young sharks develop by one of three different strategies, although in all cases the eggs, after fertilization, are passed through the shell gland, where they are enclosed within a protective case.

In oviparous species, such as the hornsharks, wobbegongs and most of the catsharks, the cases are thick and leathery; these eggs are discharged from the female, usually in pairs, almost immediately. The most common shape is more or less rectangular, with long sticky tendrils at the corners for secure attachment to corals or rocks. The dimensions and shape of the egg-case and the length of the tendrils vary considerably, however, and are usually species-specific. Swellshark embryos take almost a year to develop, breathing by means of external gills in the meantime. Fullterm swellsharks possess two rows of sharp, backward-pointing denticles on the dorsal surface which are thought to help them to rupture the egg case and aid them in wriggling out of the small opening. These denticles are shed soon after hatching.

The hornsharks, however, produce extraordinary screwlike egg-cases, between 5 and 6 inches in length, with broad lateral flanges and tendrils up to 6.5 feet long extending from the tip. Female Port Jackson sharks have been observed carrying these egg-cases in their mouths and depositing them firmly in rock crevices, where the rubbery shells harden, making the eggs almost impossible to remove, and thus safe from predation The embryo within is nurtured for almost a year by the yolk-sac before it finally emerges.

Viviparous species, such as some houndsharks and most carcharhinids, including bull sharks, blue sharks and the hammerheads, have developed a highly sophisticated method of nurturing their young. The eggs hatch in the oviduct and the yolk-sac of each embryo develops into a placenta in close contact with the uterine wall. The embryo is connected to the placenta by an umbilical cord, through which oxygen and nutrients derived from the blood of the mother are conveyed to the young shark. This is not unlike the reproductive strategy practised by mammals, the most advanced creatures on earth's evolutionary scale.

Ovoviviparous species, which account for the majority of living sharks, produce eggs in thin-walled cases which hatch within the uterus. Here the developing embryos are nourished by huge yolk-sacs and the pups are not released until they are capable of fending for themselves. Most of the Lamniform sharks are thought to conform to this reproductive system, as well as some carcharhinids. No placental connection is formed, but some species may be nourished by a secretion from the lining of the uterus known appropriately as "uterine milk."

Another curious feature of some ovoviviparous species is known as intrauterine cannibalism. Female sand tigers are known to produce large numbers of pea-sized eggs. Following fertilization several eggs in each oviduct hatch, but the most aggressive embryo then proceeds to devour its siblings. The female continues to ovulate to provide food for the developing shark pup, which is born when it attains a length of about 29 inches. A similar phenomenon is thought to occur in threshers, makos, the porbeagle and the salmon shark, although in these species between one and six embryos hatch, feeding on the steady stream of eggs produced by the mother. A 16-foot female thresher may give birth to between one and six pups each measuring an incredible 47 inches, although half of this is tail, and well able to fend for itself in the outside world.

The fact remains that we are remarkably ill-informed as to the reproductive details of most shark species. Since only a single gravid great white shark has been caught to date, much has yet to be learned regarding litter size and the proportions of the pups at birth, although it is thought that, like most lamniform sharks, litters rarely exceed four pups, each around 23 inches in length. Similarly gravid basking sharks have never been encountered, despite the fact that this is a species which is commonly exploited for its large liver.

There is also considerable controversy surrounding the whale shark's method of reproduction. In 1953 in the Gulf of Mexico, a single egg-case was found containing an almost fullterm embryo: a 14 inches replica of the world's largest fish, right down to the checkerboard pattern. More recently, however, young whale sharks have been caught which show distinct umbilical scars, suggesting that vivipary is the normal state of affairs, and that the egg-case was a freak.

In ovoviviparous and viviparous species the young sharks are usually born tail-first, although young hammerheads are delivered headfirst, with the pliable winglike extensions of the head folded back. The enlarged denticles which line the edges of the sawshark pup's elongated rostrum are soft at birth, so as not to damage the mother and the sharp dorsal spines of the spiny dogfish pups are capped with knobs of cartilage for the same reason, these being shed soon after birth.

Shark pups are not born until they are capable of fending for themselves; there are no known instances of postnatal parental care. The gestation period varies greatly between species, that of the tope or school shark being one of the shortest known, at around six months. By contrast, the gestation period of the spiny dogfish is one of the longest known for any vertebrate, the development of the pups sometimes extending over two years. There is some evidence that the gestation period of the basking shark may be even longer, but further research is necessary.

The number of young produced varies from species to species, but litters rarely exceed 100 pups and are usually much smaller. The size of the pups is not necessarily correlated to the size of the parent, or even to the maximum size to which the species may grow. Generally speaking, however, pups which are large in proportion to their mother are few in number per litter.

Information is available for only a few sharks species, generally those that are exploited in some way commercially, or favoured by game fishermen. Most viviparous sharks bear between six and twelve young, although hammerheads commonly produce litters of up to 40. Other species with large litters include the tiger shark, in which sixty or more pups are produced, each measuring around 23 inches, and blue sharks, in which an average of 70 pups each measuring around 17 inches. A 16-foot female bluntnose sixgill shark may produce up to 100 pups, each between 23 and 27 inches long.

Despite man's primeval fear of being eaten alive, which has been exploited with great financial success by the film industry, every year only around 100 reports are received of people being attacked by sharks. Detailed studies of these attacks over a number of years has revealed that the great majority of shark attacks take place in water which is at more than 68°F and more than half within 200 feet of the shore or at the surface of the water. Of course, as we have seen, there are species such as the tiger shark which specifically prefer such warm, shallow waters, but the statistics also indicate very accurately the conditions under which most people are in the water: close to the beach and in the summer in temperate regions or all year round in the tropics.

Fewer than 20 percent of all known shark species have been directly implicated in, or are suspected of, attacks on humans. The most dangerous species by far are the great white, tiger, nurse and bull sharks. The oceanic whitetip is also highly suspect, especially in instances where large numbers of people find themselves in the water after accidents on the high seas. About twenty other species have also been known to attack humans, including sand tigers, Pacific and Atlantic angelsharks, makos, blue and lemon sharks and spotted and tasselled wobbegongs, although most of these are unaggressive species unless provoked. In addition, the colossal basking and whale sharks may inadvertently endanger human life by ramming boats.

Why do sharks attack humans? Various motives have been suggested, including sexual aggression and defense of territories, although, with respect to the latter, sharks defend a moving personal space rather than a fixed geographical point. Extremely high levels of testosterone have been detected in bull and Caribbean reef sharks during the breeding season, which in all probability make them particularly aggressive. Silky sharks and grey reef sharks have recently been shown to possess a complicated range of threat postures, usually involving an arched back, raised snout and lowered tail and pectoral fins, which may relate to space intrusion. These postures are undoubtedly recognized by other sharks as danger signals, which consequently back off, although divers are unlikely to perceive the significance of such actions and may suffer an attack as a result.

A more common motive is undoubtedly the instinctive search for food which takes up much of the shark's time. Sharks have been present on this earth for eons, whereas man's occupation of the planet is by comparison very recent, thus it is not possible that sharks could have evolved specifically to take advantage of man as a prey item. It is commonly believed today that a shark attack on a human being is a case of mistaken identity.

Each year about 15 people are attacked by great white sharks; some two-thirds of the victims subsequently die. Great whites are among the few sharks that regularly prey on marine mammals, especially seals. One theory is that divers and bathers present an aspect not unlike that of an abnormal, clumsy seal in general outline and actions, and since most predators are programmed to instinctively seek out wounded or sick animals, it is not perhaps surprising that sharks are stimulated to attack.

However, the fact remains that, even among habitual swimmers in areas of high risk such as Australia and South Africa, the probability of being attacked by a shark is very low. It has been estimated that the risk of drowning near a bathing beach is over 1,000 times greater than the probability of being the victim of a shark's miscalculation. If these figures are not reassuring enough, the option is to stay out of the water. There are to date no records of sharks attacking humans on dry land!

To look at it from another point of view, far more sharks are dispatched by humans every year than vice versa. The world's commercial catch of sharks, skates and rays currently exceeds 600,000 tons per year, while in the United States the shark fishing industry grosses over $5 million per year, with carcharhinids (37,500 tons per year) and spiny dogfishes (42,000 tons per year) accounting for the majority of catches.

What are these sharks used for? Basking sharks, with their surface-feeding habits and large bulk, once occupied a prominent place in the world's shark fishing industry, although today carcharhinids and squalids are more important. Virtually no part of this gargantuan beast goes to waste. An average-sized basking shark will yield around a ton of pinkish, boneless meat while its liver generates up to 900 litres of oil. The fins are removed for the preparation of shark-fin soup, the flesh is smoked, fried, or minced for use in fishburgers and the skeleton is baked in a huge oven and later ground up for animal feed and fertilizer. But it is the liver-oil of this and other sharks which has the greatest worth.

Until the 1950s shark-liver oil was valued as a major source of vitamin A, although the advent of a cheaper synthetic alternative has today rendered this industry more or less obsolete. Shark-liver oil was also once used to lubricate fine machinery, and although synthetic substitutes are now available there is still little to beat the shark-derived product at high altitudes. The liver of deep-sea sharks is also rich in an oil known as squalene, which is widely used in the cosmetics industry as a skin softener and protector. In addition, the Japanese consider squalene to be a cure for everything from cancer to heart attacks; it is marketed as small capsules known as "marine gold," which sell at around 1,500 dollars per kilogram.

Although in Asian and South Sea Island communities shark meat has always formed a large part of the dietary protein, it is only recently, with the growing need to feed the burgeoning world population, that sharks are becoming widely used as a food species in the western world. Today porbeagles are popular in Italy, catsharks in France, makos and threshers in California and blacktips in Florida, while in Britain more than 12,000 tons of spiny dogfish are landed annually to supply the demands of the fish and chip trade, and sold under the pseudonym of "rock salmon" or "flake."

Other uses of shark products include the manufacture of wallets, handbags and belts from the strong leather produced by tanning the hide. The untanned skin, complete with denticles, was once highly valued among cabinet-makers as a type of sandpaper known as shagreen, and is still used today for samurai sword hilts. Thousands of dogfish find their way onto the dissecting table every year, thus assisting in the training of zoology students the world over. In primitive societies shark teeth have long been used as tools and weapons, while today they are highly valued as jewellery and ornaments in the western world. A tooth of a great white shark, for example, may fetch up to $200 if mounted as a pendant, while a full set of jaws from a large specimen is currently worth up to 7,000 dollars in Australia.

Some of the larger sharks are regarded as exceptional sport by game fishermen. Of particular value are species such as makos, which leap from the water in an attempt to rid themselves of the line, while the prestige associated with single-handedly hauling a large great white from the water is eagerly sought by some fishermen. In recent years the increase in popularity of such sports is having a considerable impact on shark numbers. In 1965, only 2,600 tons of pelagic sharks were landed by game fishermen in the western Atlantic, a figure which had increased to a phenomenal 15,900 tons by 1980.

Current medical opinion is that sharks may have a lot to offer. It has recently been discovered that sharks rarely get cancer and tests have shown that their cartilage contains substances which inhibit the development of tumours implanted in laboratory animals. Another component of shark cartilage, known as chondroiten, has been tested for the manufacture of artificial skin for burn patients and shark corneas have been used to replace damaged corneas in human eyes. In addition, the liver-oil contains a substance known as co-enzyme Q10, which may also have anti-carcinogenic properties.

Sharks have recently come into their own as the star attractions of diving tours, especially in island cultures where tourism is the main source of income. In addition they are also popular with aquaria; with the increase in knowledge of shark biology, many species now survive in captivity. A favourite species with the public is the sand tiger, whose mouth literally bristles with teeth. Up to 15,000 people a day visit the Shark Encounter Tank at Sea World, Florida, where several species of shark can be viewed from a glass-enclosed conveyor belt which passes through the middle of the aquarium.

Sharks are among the most successful of all underwater predators. They are situated at the top of the ocean food chain and as such have few natural enemies other than a larger shark and a wide range of parasites. In all ecosystems, both terrestrial and aquatic, such so-called "apex predators" are present in small numbers as compared to the numbers of organisms at lower levels in the food chain. For example, it is estimated that for every 100,000 sharks taken by the Florida fishery, only 27 are great whites, while between 1957 and 1983, a paltry 76 great whites were caught in the western Atlantic.

An additional problem is that even the smallest shark species reproduce very slowly. As an example, male spiny dogfish do not become sexually mature until about 11 years old, while the females reach breeding age at an incredible 19 or 20 years. Their litters are small, ranging on average between four and seven pups and the gestation period may last up to two years. Although these small sharks are thought to live for anything up to a century, it is clear that overfished populations could take decades to recover, if at all.

In recent years the increased demand for food to support the burgeoning human population has led to the expansion of shark fisheries, although the Food and Agriculture Organization considers only about 7% of shark species to be of major importance commercially. In 1975, California's commercial fisheries landed less than half a million tons of sharks, a figure which had increased sevenfold by 1985.

Unfortunately, examples of the commercial overexploitation of sharks already exist. Achill Island, off the west coast of Ireland, was the site of a thriving industry based on basking sharks in the 1950s and 1960s, up to 1,500 of these colossal fish being taken annually as they cruised close to the shore in the breeding season. A gradual reduction in numbers during the 1970s caused no undue alarm, but today the industry has ground to a complete halt. The local basking shark population has been completely wiped out.

Notwithstanding this poignant example of overfishing, the annual harvest of basking sharks in European waters is still almost certainly exceeding the reproductive capacity of this species. In 1979 fishermen of the European Community and Norway slaughtered 2,266 basking sharks, but in 1986 only 493 were taken. Of those taken females outnumbered males by a ratio of 30 or 40 to one, and most showed signs of recent sexual activity. Thus not only is the current population being threatened, but the next as well.

In Australian waters game fishing is taking its toll on the large, predatory species which confer the greatest kudos among aficionados of the sport. It is suggested that almost half of the sexually mature female great whites have been lost during the past five years. Despite the fact that South Australian waters, particularly the region known as Dangerous Reef, contain a higher concentration of great whites than anywhere else in the world, the 200 or so killed in the past 40 years has put a considerable strain on the population. Scientists and local fishermen alike consider that the presence of 40 great whites in the area is an optimistic estimate and that even if the species was completely protected, recovery would be a slow process.

In attempts to counter the possibility of shark attack, beaches in high risk areas such as southeast Australia and the Natal coast of South Africa have been divided from the open sea by overlapping, weighted gill nets positioned parallel to the shore. Since sharks are unable to swim backwards, once trapped in these nets they rapidly drown; the nets must be inspected regularly for damage, and their cargo of dead sharks extracted. The price paid for such shark-free bathing, however, is high. Statistics over sixteen years pertaining to the Queensland nets make depressing reading. Not only did these nets trap over 20,500 sharks, including many species which are not remotely dangerous to man, but 465 dugongs, 317 porpoises, 2,654 sea turtles and 10,889 rays also became entangled and died.

Sharks have long suffered from poor public relations in the world of man, but at last they are beginning to find friends among their two-legged cohabitants of this planet. The barbaric slaughter of over 100,000 carcharhinid sharks off the coast of Florida earlier this year, when the fins were sliced from the living fish and the worthless remains cast back into the sea to die a slow and agonizing death, provoked a howl of outrage among the general public. Endangered shark species are slowly finding their way onto lists of animals protected by international legislation. The plight of the great white, for example, is considered to be so aggravated by the trade in souvenirs, that it has been proposed for inclusion on Appendix 1 of the Convention on International Trade in Endangered Species of Wild Fauna and Flora (CITES), whereby trade in any part of this shark would be prohibited.

Sharks have occupied the seas of the world for close to 400 million years. For much of this time these graceful yet death-dealing fish ruled supreme in their undersea kingdom, but as man has come to dominate the planet they have suffered increasingly from the invasion of their domain. Supertankers and submarines now traverse wide expanses of ocean previously inhabited only by organic life, large sharks are relentlessly persecuted so that man can immerse himself in the warm coastal seas for pleasure and the oceans are increasingly coming to resemble the sewers of the world as we rid ourselves of the unwanted byproducts of human "civilization."

Aside from the ethical question as to our right to annihilate our fellow species on this planet, if we exterminate the shark, either inadvertently or by design, who knows in what way we might disastrously alter the natural ecological balance of the seas.

The policy of protecting Sydney's beaches with offshore shark nets has been in successful operation for more than fifty years. However, in some areas, such as nearby Botany Bay, the enormous expense of establishing and maintaining similar defenses makes them unfeasible and the authorities can do little more than warn prospective swimmers and divers of the risks of taking to the water (above).

The great white shark (right), owing to its impressive array of gleaming white, razor-sharp teeth, has been elevated to star status by the horror film industry. Although a voracious predator, the great white's reputation as an indiscriminate man-eater is largely unjustified; it is merely doing what Nature intended, in much the same way as the lion, pre-eminent carnivore of the African savanna, does.

A tried and tested way of attracting sharks
to a particular area is a process known as
'chumming'. The bait varies greatly, from
chopped-up mackerel to slaughterhouse
blood and offal. The rapidity with which
sharks, in this case a great white
accompanied by a host of small bony fish,
appear is testimony to their enhanced
olfactory senses.

Despite having been the victim of a horrific attack by a great white shark, Australian diver Rodney Fox today dedicates much of his time to the conservation of the species, which is rapidly disappearing from South Australian waters. Trophy-hunting game fishermen are largely to blame for this decline, especially as a set of jaws can fetch as much as 4,000 dollars on the open market.

The great white shark (left) occurs in all tropical, subtropical and temperate seas, including the Mediterranean. It usually frequents relatively shallow offshore waters, although its range extends from the surf line of shallow bays to depths in excess of 3,900 feet.

Although its natural prey also includes bony fish, squid, dolphins and other sharks, the great white has a noted predilection for seals and sealions. A floating dummy attracting the attention of a great white (above) lends weight to the theory that the silhouette of a swimmer or diver resembles that of the shark's favourite pinniped prey.

Another method used to attract sharks, in this case a great white, is to suspend baits of meat or fish on the surface of the water. The shark is, in effect, attacking blind, as its eyes roll back in their sockets to protect them from the flailing claws of seals, its usual prey.

Shark cages provide an invaluable means of
studying sharks in their natural habitat
without endangering the researcher's life
and limb. Note the characteristic black eye
of the great white, and the prominent
ampullae of Lorenzini, or electrosensory
organs, on its snout.

Recent work has shown that the ampullae of Lorenzini are even able to detect the faint electrical fields produced by the reaction between metals and sea-water. This discovery provided a possible explanation of why sharks frequently bite the bars of shark cages in preference to nearby bait – behavior that had long puzzled researchers.

The great white shark is one of the few
species habitually to raise its head out of the
water, although the difference in the
refractive indices of water and air make it
unlikely that the shark can distinguish
objects above the surface with any clarity.

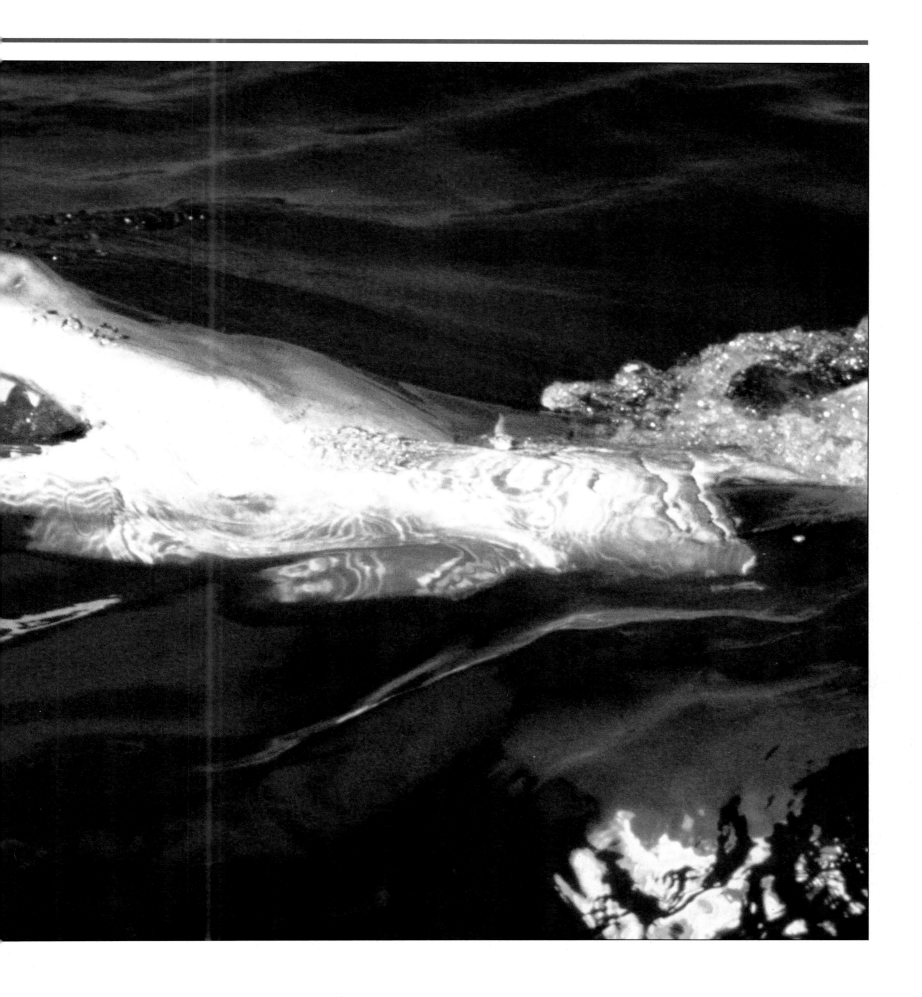

The mouth of the great white shark lies well beneath the head and only the teeth in the lower jaw are usually visible. However, when the shark attacks, the snout is lifted and the jaws are projected forwards, which increases the gape substantially and brings the upper and lower teeth into line. All 'sharklike' predatory sharks feed in a similar manner.

The great white, like all sharks, has several rows of teeth in operation at any one time. The loss of a tooth during feeding is merely temporary, since ranks of fully-formed teeth lie within the gums and gradually work their way into a vertical operational position.

Although commonly known as the great white shark, the topside of most mature individuals is usually a dull lead-gray or bluish colour, changing abruptly to off-white or cream below. Blue pointer, as the species is called in South Africa, is perhaps the more appropriate name.

Despite its formidable jaw armature and reputation, the great white shark is nevertheless a streamlined and graceful creature, supremely adapted to its role as the pre-eminent predator of the oceans.

GREAT WHITE SHARK

The great white shark is the largest
predatory fish still in existence. Although its
size is often greatly exaggerated, the largest
specimens can measure some twenty-three
feet from the tip of their blunt, conical
snouts to the more or less equal lobes of
their tails.

The mako shark is a solitary, open-ocean
species found in temperate and tropical seas
around the world. One of the fastest of all
fish, it is also capable of making prodigious
leaps clean out of the water, and is thus
greatly prized by game fishermen. Note the
parasitic copepods, with trailing egg-strings,
on the dorsal fin of the above specimen.

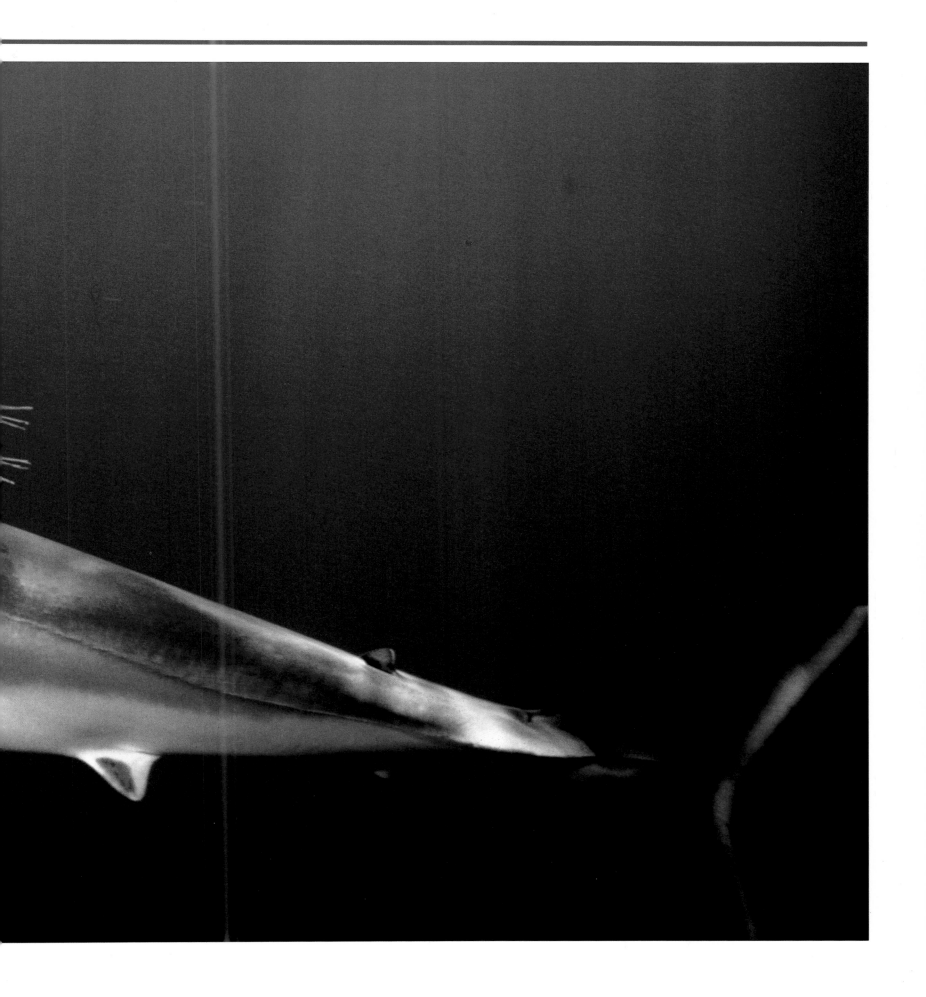

Makos, which attain a maximum length of
between ten and thirteen feet, have the
narrow, hooked teeth characteristic of those
sharks that feed predominantly on fish. As
in other mackerel sharks, the upper and
lower lobe of the tail fin are almost equal.
'Mako' is the Maori word for shark.

The sand tiger, also known as the gray nurse or spotted raggedtooth shark, is a stout-bodied species found in the Atlantic, Indian and west Pacific Oceans where it favors shallow water. Like the mako it is a fish-eating shark, as its protruding, spike-like teeth indicate.

The swellshark is an oviparous species and each egg is enclosed in a large, thick-walled case that protects it during development. One study found, however, that more than half the embryos fell victim to carnivorous marine molluscs.

This swellshark egg case has been opened to reveal the embryo at a very early stage of its development, throughout which it is nourished by the yolk sac. The young embryos obtain oxygen by means of feathery external gills.

Below: at seven months the embryo is almost ready to emerge from the egg case. One characteristic of the swellsharks is that the young possess a double row of enlarged, hooked denticles on the head and dorsal surface to assist the young shark in levering itself out of the egg case.

Swellsharks are so named because, when threatened, they can inflate their bodies with air or water, which makes them either impossible to prize free from rock crevices or, if they have been surprised in the open, too large, hopefully, to be swallowed. Swellsharks are a sluggish, nocturnal species and may reach up to 3.3 feet in length.

During copulation the male smallspotted catshark winds his body completely around that of the female. Later, she lays about twenty eggs, whose rectangular egg cases measure some two by four inches. The cases possess long tendrils to anchor them to seaweed or rocks. The embryos take between eight and nine months to develop, before emerging as fully-formed sharks, albeit only four inches long.

The smallspotted catshark, also commonly known as the lesser spotted dogfish, is essentially a North Atlantic and Mediterranean species that rarely exceeds three feet in length. It is a bottom-dwelling shark that feeds mainly on molluscs and crustaceans. Its best-known contribution to science has perhaps been via the zoology student's dissection table.

Individual gray reef sharks are common in shallow lagoons and near coral reefs in the Indian and west Pacific Oceans, especially around Australia. For this reason, it is one of the most photographed of the requiem sharks.

Although very similar in general outline to
many other requiem sharks, gray reef sharks,
also appropriately known as long-nosed
blacktail sharks, may be identified by the
black margins on their pectoral and tail fins
and the white-smudged, rounded dorsal fin.

Gray reef sharks have the small round eyes and underslung mouths characteristic of requiem sharks. Mature specimens are usually around six feet long, although individuals of around eight feet are not unknown.

Gray Reef Shark

Although gray reef sharks are usually found in loose aggregations of between twenty and thirty individuals either where reefs drop off into the open ocean or near the ocean floor, solitary individuals are more common in the shallow waters over coral reefs and in lagoons.

The behavior of the gray reef shark is
actually better documented than its general
biology. When the shark is intimidated, it
performs a series of 'threat postures', in
which the back is arched, the snout raised
and the pectoral fins lowered. If the
intimidator does not take heed, it may be
pursued and attacked.

Some coral reef localities, such as those around the Maldives in the Indian Ocean, are becoming increasingly popular as places where visiting divers can 'feed' gray reef sharks.

Gray reef sharks are sexually mature at about
seven years of age. They are viviparous,
producing small litters of up to six pups after
a gestation period of about a year.

Gray Reef Shark

Gray reef sharks are often seen in the company of shoals of small bony fish, which they make no attempt to eat. Some researchers have suggested that these bony fish may act as cleaners, keeping the sharks' skin free of ectoparasites.

The silky shark, so called because its smaller, flatter denticles give it a smoother skin, is one of the commonest of open-ocean sharks. It is a circumtropical, fish-feeding shark which grows to a maximum of eleven feet. Like the gray reef shark, it adopts 'threat postures' when intimidated.

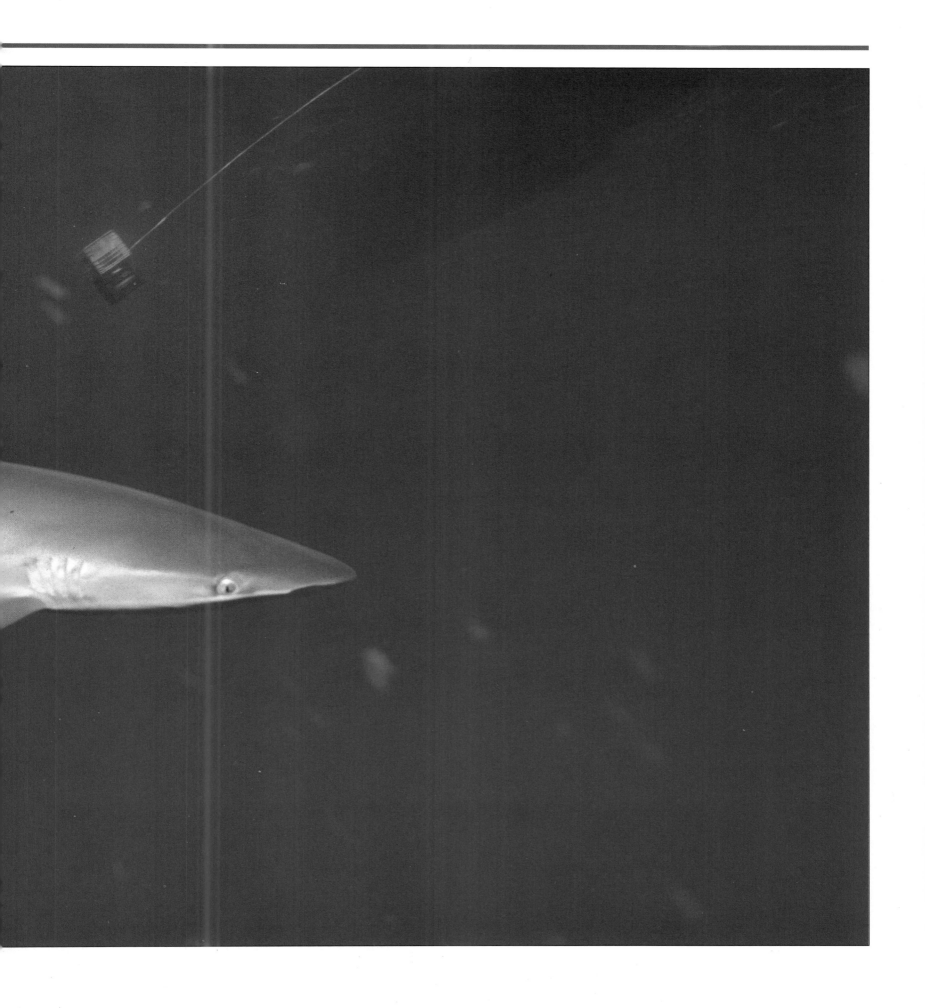

The bull shark, a cosmopolitan species
found in both tropical and temperate
shallow seas, is a voracious predator with a
predilection for young sharks, even those of
the same species. It is frequently found in
estuaries, attracted by the debris emanating
from rivers, and is noted for its ability to live
quite happily in freshwater lakes and rivers.

The sandbar shark favors similar habitats to the bull shark, which makes it a prime candidate for predation by the latter. It is a stout-bodied shark whose name reflects its preference for a shallow habitat with a sandy or muddy bottom. Mature individuals are about six and a half feet long, and they can be distinguished from the larger bull sharks by their large, erect first dorsal fins.

Oceanic Whitetip Shark

The oceanic whitetip is an almost cosmopolitan shark, although it does prefer waters in excess of 70°F and over 650 feet deep. It is seen here in the company of several pilot fish, small teleosts that were once thought to lead sharks to their prey, but are now known to dance attendance on the larger fish in order to scavenge any leftovers when they feed.

Rarely found close to the shore, the oceanic whitetip is not normally considered a dangerous species, although it is often first on the scene after an accident on the high seas and has been implicated in attacks on survivors in these situations. Oceanic whitetips are identified by the prominent, white-mottled tips to their fins, including the huge, rounded first dorsal.

Although such fast-swimming bony fish as marlin, barracuda and tuna commonly feature in its diet, the oceanic whitetip is considered to be a lazy species, hunting by guile rather than in prolonged bursts of speed. The whitetip is also known to feed on seabirds, marine turtles, mammalian carrion and garbage.

The blacktip reef shark is a small, rather slender fish distinguished by and named after its black-tipped fins and tail. It frequents coral reefs and shallow lagoons in the Indian and west Pacific Oceans. Interestingly, it has increased its range to include the eastern Mediterranean since the construction of the Suez Canal.

Blacktip reef sharks have narrow-cusped teeth, ideal for a diet that includes small sharks, bony fish and octopus. Blacktips reach a maximum length of about six and a half feet and are considered to be nonaggressive to man.

The Caribbean reef shark occurs in the
shallow inshore waters of both the west
Atlantic Ocean and, as its name suggests,
the Caribbean Sea, especially around the
coral reefs of the West Indies. Tagging the
dorsal fin enables researchers to monitor the
shark's migration patterns using capture-
recapture techniques.

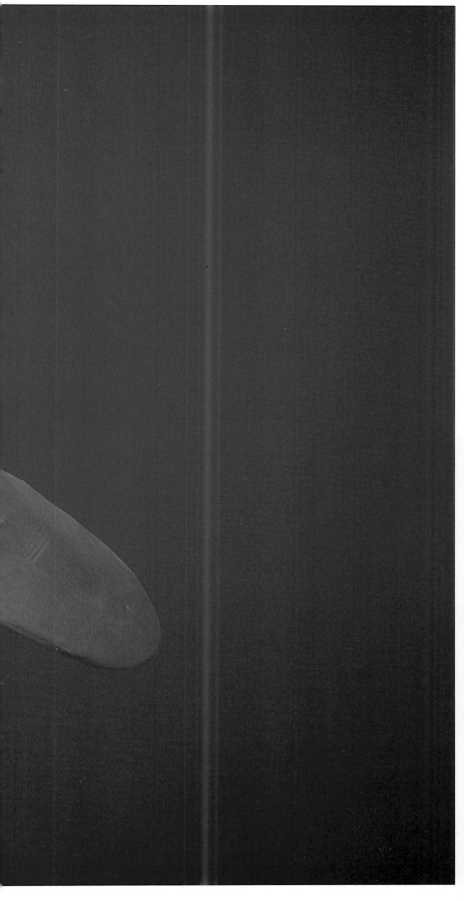

Caribbean reef sharks attain a maximum length of around ten feet and are known to have been involved in several attacks on divers. They are not infrequently encountered lying motionless on the sea floor or in underwater caves, in total contradiction to the old belief that sharks must swim perpetually to obtain oxygen, or die.

Tiger sharks, like Caribbean reef sharks, have been found in a torpid state in underwater caves. It has been suggested that highly oxygenated freshwater currents peculiar to these caves may help to rid the sharks of external marine parasites. Tiger sharks possess the spiracles that are characteristic of true benthic sharks and through which a current of water can be drawn to oxygenate the gills while the shark lies motionless on the bottom.

The tiger shark is second only to the great white in size, in voracity and in its reputation for attacking man. Individuals of over sixteen feet are common. The characteristic vertical stripes from which the species gets its name are only well developed in young sharks and fade in individuals over ten feet.

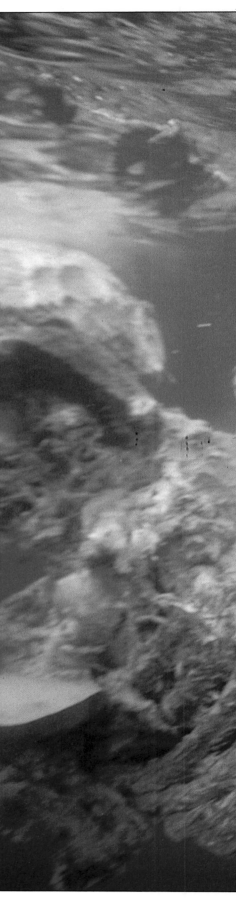

The tiger shark is probably the most opportunistic feeder of all sharks. As it feeds on a whale carcass, the tiger shark churns up the surrounding water with violent sideways movements of its tail and the rear part of its body. These movements are necessary to move the shark's jaws in a sawlike manner through the flesh, thus enabling it to detach a mouthful.

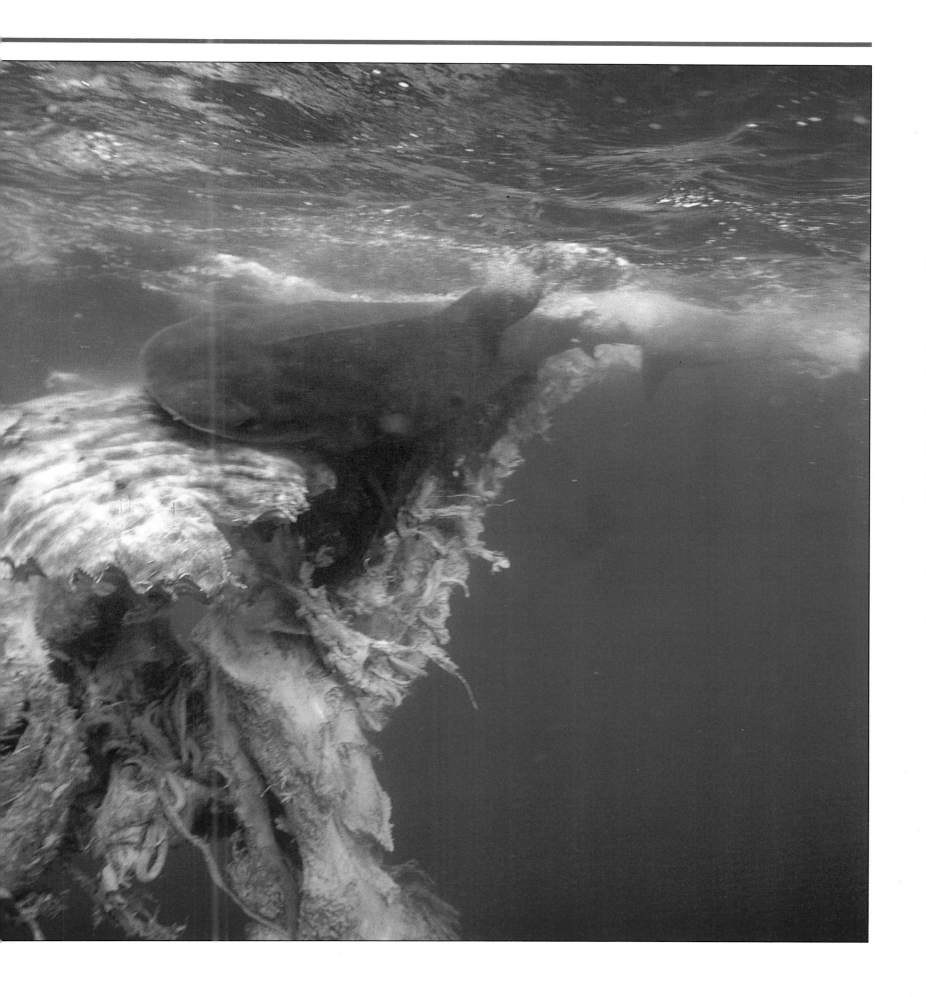

The University of Miami has long been
engaged in studying sharks in their natural
habitat. Researchers are here tagging a
young tiger shark before releasing it so as to
monitor its future movements.

During courtship, male sharks of many species are known to use their teeth to grasp the female behind the first dorsal fin. This female tiger shark bears scars as evidence of this practice. As protection, female sharks often have thicker skin in this region than males of the same species.

Tiger sharks are typified by their huge bulk, colored gray-green above and white below. They are circumtropical fish, found both in coastal and offshore seas and occurring from the surf line to waters about 460 feet deep.

TIGER SHARK

Tiger sharks have unusually wide mouths,
containing rows of large, asymmetrical and
saw-edged teeth, resembling cockscombs in
overall shape. These are not normally visible
until the shark attacks. This particular tiger
shark is host to a parasitic copepod in the
corner of its mouth.

The tiger shark, like the great white, lies at
the top of the ocean food chain, so,
although widespread in tropical seas, it is
not truly common anywhere. Unfortunately,
its popularity with anglers, combined with
the toll exacted by shark nets, means that
the already small populations are decreasing
faster than they can reproduce themselves.

Lemon sharks have a much greater tolerance of high water temperatures and low oxygen concentration than other sharks, which enables them to survive in the shallow lagoons of the Bahamas. These lagoons are commonly used as nursery grounds, as they provide the juvenile sharks with some protection from large predators.

The young lemon sharks remain in these waters, gradually increasing their range, until they reach sexual maturity at about seven years old. The difference between the yearling lemon shark (above) and the subadult (left) is principally one of size; mature individuals reach a maximum of about ten feet.

LEMON SHARK

Lemon sharks live quite happily in waters so shallow that their dorsal fins protrude from the surface of the water. They are usually found in the coastal seas of the eastern Pacific and western Atlantic Oceans.

Many species of shark are accompanied by
remoras, or sharksuckers, and lemon sharks
are no exception. Although these bony fish
are specifically adapted to attach themselves
to the shark by means of a suction disc on
top of their head, much of the time they are
free-swimming, saving energy by riding in
the shark's slipstream.

Lemon sharks are able to breathe while lying motionless on the sea's bottom by opening and closing their mouths and thus pumping water over the gill filaments where oxygen dissolved in the water is exchanged for carbon dioxide dissolved in the shark's blood. This phenomenon is also seen in bull and nurse sharks.

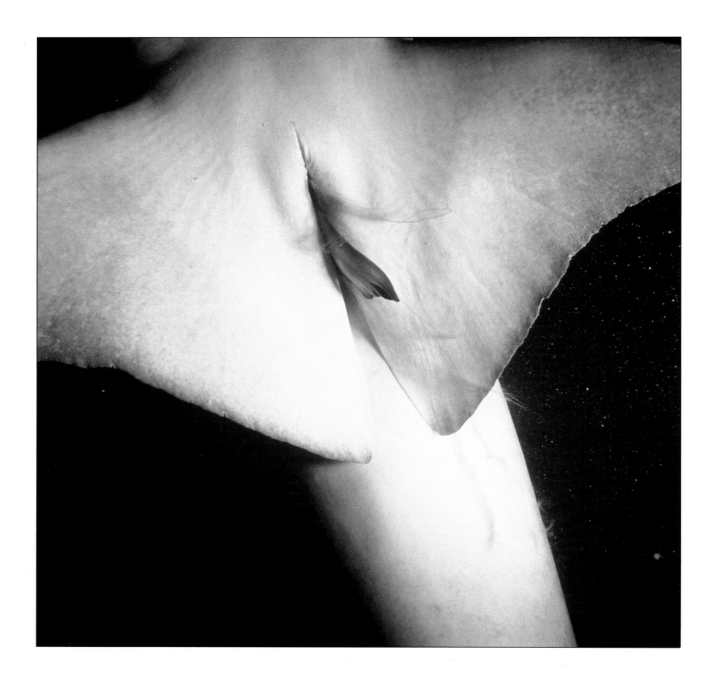

Lemon sharks are viviparous and the females
give birth to up to fifteen pups in a single
litter. During its development inside the
female each embryo receives nourishment
via an umbilical cord and a yolk sac, which
is modified into a placenta, in close contact
with the wall of the uterus.

The pups emerge tail first and are about twenty-four inches long at birth. The umbilical cord breaks as the young shark attempts to swim away, leaving a small depression in its underside, between the pectoral fins. The juvenile lemon shark is now completely independent and will receive no parental care.

Lemon Shark

The lemon shark is named after its coloration, which is yellow-brown above and pale yellow or off-white below. It is one of the most popular sharks kept in captivity and has been widely studied, especially by researchers at the University of Miami.

The blue shark is one of the more slender
species and is distinguished by a first dorsal
fin that lies well behind the long, narrow
pectorals. It is one of the most widespread of
all sharks, occurring circumglobally in both
temperate and tropical seas.

Blue sharks, also known as bluedogs or blue
whalers, have long, conical snouts with the
mouth positioned well behind the large eyes.
The maximum recorded length for a blue
shark is twelve and a half feet.

The blue shark is an appropriately named species since its dorsal surface, fins and tail are a bright indigo blue that contrasts markedly with its white belly. Known as countershading, such coloration is a common feature of pelagic fish, rendering them less visible to predators when seen either from above, against a dark background, or from below, against the light.

Although essentially open-ocean pelagic
fish, blue sharks sometimes frequent inshore
areas, especially where the continental shelf
is narrow. They are often seen swimming
lazily at the surface, but, using acoustic
telemetry, they have been tracked diving
down to about 1600 feet.

Male blue sharks mature at four to five years old and females about a year later. They are viviparous, the young being born after a gestation period of up to a year, and litters vary greatly in size from as few as four pups to as many as 135. The blue shark's average lifespan is about twenty years.

BLUE SHARK

Blue sharks are renowned for their extensive migrations. Information from tagging studies has revealed that one North Atlantic individual travelled almost 3,800 miles from the New York area to the Brazilian coast, while journeys across the Atlantic Ocean, from west to east, have also been recorded.

Blue sharks have a reputation for attacking divers, especially spearfishermen with trophies in tow. Nevertheless, lone individuals often display curiosity rather than aggression and may allow themselves to be fed.

Chumming rapidly attracts large numbers of blue sharks. This species is renowned for its feeding frenzies, which are thought to occur when the sharks' senses are overloaded with olfactory and auditory signals. Blue sharks frequently cause havoc among large hauls of fish, destroying nets and even attacking boats.

Acknowledging the potential threat of close
encounters with blue sharks, marine
researchers usually work in pairs so as to
ensure that other blues, attracted by the
activity, do not catch the diver unawares.

Blue sharks have a broad-based diet, feeding
on sardines and other herring-like fish, eels,
flying fish, sea birds, members of the cod
family, tuna, small sharks, squid and
cetacean carrion. They also habitually
follow boats in the hope of easy pickings.

The narrow, slightly hooked teeth of the blue shark give it an excellent grip on slippery prey, such as mackerel. Blue sharks are a favorite with anglers as the species puts up a good fight, often leaping clear of the water.

The 'Neptunic', a suit comprising about 400,000 stainless steel rings, was developed by researchers to make shark investigation an altogether less hazardous occupation. Although the suit prevents shark teeth from penetrating through to the diver's skin, heavy bruising can still occur.

The Atlantic sharpnose is, as its name
suggests, a shark of the northwest Atlantic
Ocean and also of the Caribbean Sea,
frequenting, often in large numbers, shallow
coastal waters and estuaries. It is also able to
enter fresh water, but never ventures far
from the sea.

Despite being a requiem shark, the Atlantic sharpnose is of modest proportions, attaining a maximum length of a little over three feet. A broad, flat snout and large eyes are distinctive features of this small, harmless shark.

107

A surface-dwelling species of the open
ocean, the blue shark pursues its piscine prey
at speeds of up to forty miles an hour.

The timid, largely nocturnal whitetip reef shark is distinguished by the conspicuous white markings on the extremities of all its fins. This six-and-a-half-foot-long shark is found in the tropical Indian and Pacific Oceans, often around coral reefs, at depths ranging from twenty-six to 130 feet. The whitetip is primarily a fish-feeder, and uses its extremely short, broad snout to extract its prey from reef crevices.

Scalloped hammerheads are found throughout the world in all seas except the very coldest. This is the commonest of the hammerheads, and it reaches a maximum length of over thirteen feet. During the day scalloped hammerheads often congregate in schools of about a hundred, dispersing at night to feed singly. It is not yet known whether the schools are associated with mating or social behaviour or whether they serve as protection against even larger fish.

Bonnetheads are the least extreme of all the hammerheads, having simply a broad, shovel-shaped head rather than the extended 'wings' characteristic of other members of the family. Like scalloped hammmerheads, bonnetheads also form schools, but only at irregular intervals and always at the surface; the purpose of such aggregations is also unknown.

Bonnetheads have an interesting distribution, and occur in tropical regions of both the east Pacific and the west Atlantic Oceans. This suggests that the species was widespread before the Central American land bridge formed. The maximum length of a bonnethead is around five feet.

The great hammerhead is the largest member of the family Sphyrnidae, some individuals having been measured at over twenty feet. Apart from the grotesque lateral extensions of the head, with the eyes positioned at the extremities, the basic design of all hammerheads is that of a typical requiem shark. The exact function of these 'wings' is not as yet fully understood and theories range from their potential hydrofoil effect to the possible benefits of binocular vision.

Great hammerheads are found in all temperate and tropical seas, usually in shallow waters around reefs, but occasionally they will venture offshore. Research indicates that they are partial to stingrays, although they also eat both pelagic and benthic fish. All hammerheads are viviparous, and litters of up to forty pups are common. The young are born with their 'wings' folded back.

GREAT HAMMERHEAD SHARK

Great hammerhead sharks undertake seasonal migrations, generally extending their range into temperate waters during the summer, although they are seldom ever found where the water temperature is less than 75°F.

Typically, bonnetheads are mouse-gray
above and almost white below. Their
habitual presence in shallow waters,
especially in estuaries, bays and reef habitats,
has led to their being comprehensively
studied. Biologists have discovered that this
small shark has a wide range of behavioral
postures.

Hammerheads have small mouths set well beneath the head, the small gape limiting the size of possible prey. Nevertheless, the great hammerhead, the whitefin hammerhead and the smooth hammerhead are all suspected of being dangerous to humans.

The broadnose sevengill shark, also known as the spotted sevengill cowshark, is a widespread species in temperate seas, and is particularly common in the Indo-Pacific region. In South Australian and Californian waters, the broadnose sevengill, growing to a maximum of thirteen feet, is considered to be an aggressive and potentially dangerous species.

Broadnose sevengills have large, comb-like cutting teeth in the lower jaw and single-cusped, hooked teeth in the upper jaw. This dental arrangement, located in a mouth that is much closer to the front of the head than in most sharks, means that broadnose sevengills are capable of taking a wide range of prey and they are in fact consummate omnivores.

There are thirteen species of angelshark, all of which are supremely adapted to life on the ocean floor. Their flattened bodies are blotched like the sand of the sea bottom, where angelsharks lie motionless all day, hunting only at night. Angelsharks can grow up to six and a half feet long, although most species are smaller.

Adaptation to life on the sea floor has
resulted in a remarkable resemblance
between the angelshark and another
cartilaginous species called the guitarfish,
which is in fact a ray. One clear distinction
between the two is that the angelshark's
head is clearly separated from the front
edges of the pectoral fins, whereas the
outline is continuous in rays.

This Japanese bullhead shark, a species
confined to the northwest Pacific, has been
caught by a diver for tagging. All eight
members of the family Heterodontidae
possess a sharp spine in front of each dorsal
fin and have pronounced ridges above the
eyes. The females produce screw-shaped egg
cases, which are wedged into crevices for
protection against predators.

The horn shark is found in shallow waters in the eastern Pacific. The generic name Heterodontus refers to the fact that these small, blunt-headed sharks possess both biting and crushing teeth, the latter enabling horn sharks to exploit the abundant local supply of tough-shelled benthic molluscs.

The ornate wobbegong is a bottom-dwelling
shark of the western Pacific that is
particularly common in Australian waters. It
reaches a maximum length of some ten feet
and, like all wobbegongs, has powerful jaws
lined with several rows of sharply pointed
teeth, which make it dangerous if provoked.

Wobbegongs have intricately patterned dorsal surfaces which allow them to remain undetected as they lie in ambush for the small fish, shrimps, crabs and other invertebrates that make up their diet.

Nurse sharks are a sluggish inshore species
found in shallow water in most tropical seas.
In the Atlantic they can be easily
distinguished from all other sharks by the
presence of two barbels on the underside of
the snout. These are probably used for
tactile identification of prey.

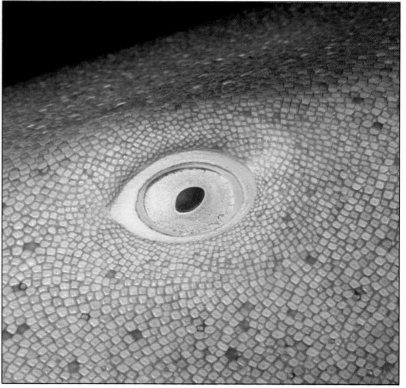

The eyes of sharks are essentially similar to those of all vertebrates; they have two types of light receivers: rods and cones. This means that, in theory, they have both daytime and night-time vision and may even be able to detect color. It is probable, however, that sluggish, shallow-water species, such as the nurse shark, whose eye is shown above, have less acute vision than the active, predatory open-ocean sharks.

Unlike most sharks, which need to keep
swimming to pass water through their gills
to obtain oxygen, nurse sharks are able to lie
motionless on the sea bottom and pump
water over their gills by opening and closing
their mouths. During the day, nurse sharks
are sometimes found piled in underwater
caves in untidy heaps comprising several
dozen individuals.

Nurse sharks and their close relatives have a unique manner of feeding that involves literally sucking their prey into their huge mouth cavities. They are generally an unaggressive species but, if provoked, they can inflict serious wounds with their small but razor-sharp teeth.

Like many bottom-dwelling sharks, the
nurse shark has a sinuous, eel-like manner of
swimming, aided by its broad, almost linear,
tail. Nurse sharks grow to a maximum length
of about ten feet and have been known to
live for up to twenty-five years in captivity.

Although the flesh of the nurse shark can be eaten, it is the thick, tough hide which is considered more valuable, both as leather and as shagreen, a type of sandpaper. Brazilian fishermen use its earstones, or otoliths, as a diuretic.

The zebra shark is an unmistakable species
with prominent longitudinal ridges along its
body, nasal barbels, a mouth situated well in
front of its tiny eyes and an arrow-like tail
which comprises almost half the shark's total
length. Zebra sharks are also often
accompanied by sharksuckers.

Zebra sharks frequently grow to more than
ten feet in length and are widespread in the
tropical regions of the Indian and west
Pacific Oceans. The tawny background and
regular dark spots of the adult zebra shark
are very different from the young
individual's vivid black and yellow stripes
from which the species gets its name.

135

ZEBRA SHARK

A bottom-dwelling species of shallow, inshore waters, the zebra shark is able to squirm into reef crevices to extract the octopuses, shelled molluscs, crustaceans and small fish on which it feeds. It is oviparous, the purplish-black egg cases having tufts of fine tendrils as anchorage.

The presence of a diver gives an indication
of how vast the whale shark is. The largest
fish in the world, the plankton-feeding
whale shark has been recorded at lengths of
over thirty-nine feet, and some biologists
suggest it could even reach a phenomenal
sixty-eight feet. Almost always seen at the
surface, it has a circumtropical distribution.

With a maximum recorded length of thirty-six feet, the basking shark is only marginally shorter than the whale shark, but it is considerably less bulky. Like the whale shark, it feeds mainly on plankton, catching these microscopic organisms by passing the surface waters in through its gaping mouth and out through the sieve-like gill slits. The abundance of plankton in the water precludes photographic clarity.

Basking sharks were once common in temperate waters throughout the world, but today their overexploitation for the oil stored in their livers and for their tender flesh has led to their disappearance in some areas. Two distinct populations occur, one on either side of the equator, and it is possible that these are in fact separate species.

SCIENTIFIC RESEARCH

It is necessary to study sharks in the wild in order to understand certain of their biological and behavioral characteristics that cannot be investigated in captivity. By entering the shark's underwater realm, researchers have dispelled some of the more exaggerated myths relating to these fish and shown them to be truly fascinating creatures.

The University of Miami has been studying sharks in the wild for many years. Below: researchers inject a tiger shark with tetracycline; this does not harm the shark but provides a wealth of information about the pattern and rate of its growth.

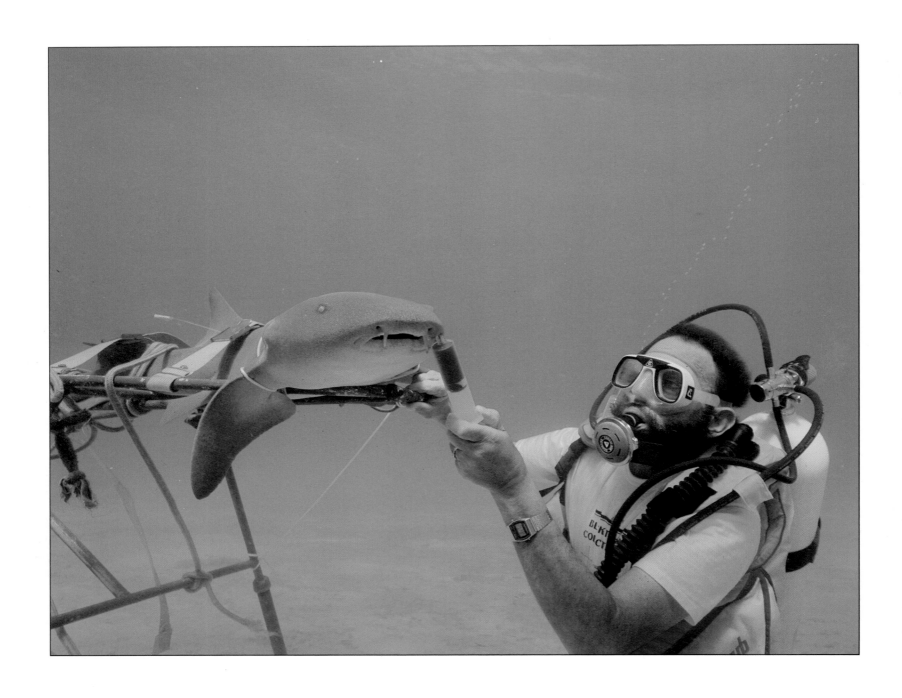

Dr Samuel H. Gruber of the University of
Miami, one of the leading figures in shark
biology and conservation, investigates the
flow of water through the olfactory system of
a nurse shark using a harmless dye.

Having been captured, this great hammerhead shark is being examined for its suitability as a study specimen. Wherever possible, sharks are not removed from the water as the lack of support for their tissues could lead to damage of the vital organs.

Shark reproduction was poorly understood
for many years, but the increasing
willingness of researchers to take to the
water to study their subject has vastly
increased knowledge in this field. The
capture of a gravid female lemon shark just
prior to her giving birth has resulted in a
unique photographic record of the delivery.

146

Many people find sharks fascinating, a fact that has only recently been recognised by the tourist industry. The shallow seas and coral reefs around the Maldives in the Indian Ocean are today the destination for expeditions of interested divers. They are able to observe gray reef sharks at close quarters and even to make contact by feeding them.

Shark cages are widely used by researchers and underwater photographers the better to study their subject without personal risk. The presence of a cage in the water is almost guaranteed to attract the attention of curious sharks in its vicinity, especially if used in conjunction with chumming techniques.

The shark suit, or 'Neptunic', was originally invented specifically to liberate researchers from the restrictions of the shark cage when observing highly predatory sharks in the wild. However, it also has potential as protection for divers in other fields who have to work in shark-infested waters.

When studying species such as the great
white, the protection of the shark cage is
vital. The huge size and awesome dentition
of this species mean that even a curious
nibble could result in fatal hemorrhaging for
the victim.

Game fishing is becoming an increasingly popular sport. Conducting shark-angling expeditions may boost the income of fishermen in coastal resorts such as those of the Adriatic (above), but there is evidence that in some areas the sport is in danger of cutting its own throat, as overfishing is depleting local shark stocks, especially those of the larger sharks, which have a very low reproduction rate.

Increasing contact with sharks in their natural habitat has helped to dispel some of the myths engendered by the film industry. Sharks are not the mindless killers portrayed on the big screen, but are complex, highly evolved creatures. Caution and respect on the part of the diver mean that even potentially dangerous species such as the tiger shark (above) can be approached without risk.

CLASSIFICATION OF LIVING SHARKS
Class: CHONDRICHTHYES
Subclass: ELASMOBRANCHII

Superorder: SQUALOMORPHII
Order: HEXANCHIFORMES (sixgill, sevengill and frilled sharks)

Family: HEXANCHIDAE (sixgills and sevengills)

Heptranchias perlo	sharpnose sevengill or perlon shark
Hexanchus griseus	bluntnose sixgill shark
Hexanchus vitulus	bigeye sixgill shark
Notorynchus cepedianus	broadnose sevengill

Family: CHLAMYDOSELACHIDAE (frilled sharks)

Chlamydoselachus anguineus	frilled shark

Order: SQUALIFORMES (dogfish sharks)
Family: ECHINORHINIDAE (bramble sharks)

Echinorhinus brucus	bramble shark
Echinorhinus cookei	prickly shark

Family: SQUALIDAE (dogfish sharks)

Aculeola nigra	hooktooth dofish
Centrophorus acus	needle dogfish
Centrophorus granulosus	gulper shark
Centrophorus harrissoni	dumb gulper shark
Centrophorus lusitanicus	lowfin gulper shark
Centrophorus moluccensis	smallfin gulper shark
Centrophorus niaukang	Taiwan gulper shark
Centrophorus squamosus	leafscale gulper shark
Centrophorus tesselatus	mosaic gulper shark
Centrophorus uyato	little gulper shark
Centroscyllium fabricii	black dogfish
Centroscyllium granulatum	granular dogfish
Centroscyllium kamoharai	bareskin dogfish
Centroscyllium nigrum	combtooth dogfish
Centroscyllium ornatum	ornate dogfish
Centroscyllium ritteri	whitefin dogfish
Centroscyllium sheikoi	rasptooth dogfish
Centroscymnus coelolepis	Portuguese dogfish
Centroscymnus crepidater	longnose velvet dogfish
Centroscymnus cryptacanthus	shortnose velvet dogfish
Centroscymnus owstoni	largespine velvet dogfish
Cirrhigaleus barbifer	mandarin dogfish
Dalatias licha	kitefin shark
Deania calcea	birdbeak dogfish
Deania histricosa	rough longnose dogfish
Deania profundorum	arrowhead dogfish
Deania quadrispinosum	longsnout dogfish
Etmopterus baxteri	New Zealand lanternshark
Etmopterus brachyurus	shorttail lanternshark
Etmopterus bullisi	lined lanternshark
Etmopterus carteri	cylindrical lanternshark
Etmopterus decacuspidatus	combtooth lanternshark
Etmopterus frontimaculatus	crow lanternshark

Etmopterus gracilispinis	broadband lanternshark
Etmopterus granulosus	southern lanternshark
Etmopterus hillianus	Caribbean lanternshark
Etmopterus lucifer	devil shark, blackbelly lanternshark
Etmopterus molleri	
Etmopterus perryi	dwarf lanternshark
Etmopterus polli	African lanternshark
Etmopterus princeps	great lanternshark
Etmopterus pusillus	smooth lanternshark
Etmopterus schmidti	darkbelly lanternshark
Etmopterus schultzi	fringefin lanternshark
Etmopterus sentosus	thorny lanternshark
Etmopterus spinax	velvet belly
Etmopterus unicolor	brown lanternshark
Etmopterus villosus	Hawaiian lanternshark
Etmopterus virens	green lanternshark
Euprotomicroides zantedeschia	taillight shark
Euprotomicrus bispinatus	pygmy shark
Heteroscymnoides marleyi	longnose pygmy shark
Isistius brasilensis	cookiecutter or cigar shark
Isistius plutodus	largetooth cookiecutter shark
Mollisquama parini	softskin dogfish
Scymnodalatias sherwoodi	Sherwood dogfish
Scymnodalatias albicauda	whitetail dogfish
Scymnodon ichiharai	Japanese velvet dogfish
Scymnodon macracanthus	longspine velvet dogfish
Scymnodon obscurus	smallmouth velvet dogfish
Scymnodon plunketi	plunket shark
Scymnodon ringens	knifetooth dogfish
Somniosus microcephalus	Greenland or sleeper shark
Somniosus pacificus	Pacific sleeper shark
Somniosus rostratus	little sleeper shark
Squaliolus aliae	smalleye pygmy shark
Squaliolus laticaudus	spined pygmy shark, cigar shark
Squalus acanthias	spiny dogfish, piked dogfish
Squalus asper	roughskin spurdog
Squalus blainvillei	longnose spurdog
Squalus cubensis	Cuban dogfish
Squalus japonicus	Japanese spurdog
Squalus megalops	shortnose spurdog
Squalus melanurus	blacktail spurdog
Squalus mitsukurii	shortspine spurdog
Squalus rancureli	Cyrano spurdog
Zameus squamulosis	velvet dogfish

Family: OXYNOTIDAE (roughsharks)

Oxynotus bruniensis	prickly dogfish
Oxynotus caribbaeus	Caribbean roughshark
Oxynotus centrina	angular roughshark
Oxynotus japonicus	Japanese roughshark
Oxynotus paradoxus	humantin, sailfin roughshark

Order: PRISTIOPHORIFORMES (sawsharks)
Family: PRISTIOPHORIDAE (sawsharks)

Pliotrema warreni	sixgill sawshark
Pristiophorus cirratus	longnose sawshark

Pristiophorus japonicus	Japanese sawshark
Pristiophorus nudipinnis	shortnose sawshark
Pristiophorus schroederi	Bahamas sawshark

Superorder: SQUATINOMORPHII

Order: SQUATINIFORMES (angelsharks)
Family: SQUATINIDAE (angelsharks, sand devils)

Squatina aculeata	sawback angelshark
Squatina africana	African angelshark
Squatina argentina	Argentine angelshark
Squatina australis	Australian angelshark
Squatina californica	Pacific angelshark
Squatina dumeril	Atlantic angelshark, sand devil
Squatina formosa	Taiwan angelshark
Squatina japonica	Japanese angelshark
Squatina nebulosa	clouded angelshark
Squatina oculata	smoothback angelshark
Squatina squatina	monkfish, angelshark
Squatina tergocellata	ornate angelshark
Squatina tergocellatoides	ocellated angelshark

Superorder: GALEOMORPHII
Order: HETERODONTIFORMES (bullhead sharks)

Family: HETERODONTIDAE (bullhead sharks, horn sharks)

Heterodontus francisci	horn shark
Heterodontus galeatus	crested bullhead shark
Heterodontus japonicus	Japanese bullhead shark
Heterodontus mexicanus	Mexican hornshark
Heterodontus portusjacksoni	Port Jackson shark
Heterodontus quoyi	Galapagos bullhead shark
Heterodontus ramalheira	whitespotted bullhead shark
Heterodontus zebra	zebra bullhead shark

Order: ORECTOLOBIFORMES (carpetsharks)
Family: PARASCYLLIDAE (collared carpetsharks)

Ciroscyllium expolitum	barbelthroat carpetshark
Ciroscyllium formosanum	Taiwan saddled carpetshark
Ciroscyllium japonicum	saddled carpetshark
Parascyllium collare	collared carpetshark
Parascyllium ferrugineum	rusty carpetshark
Parascyllium multimaculatum	Tasmanian carpetshark
Parascyllium variolatum	necklace carpetshark

Family: BRACHAELURIDAE (blind sharks)
Brachaelurus waddi	blind shark

Family: ORECTOLOBIDAE (wobbegongs)

Eucrossorhinus dasypogon	tasselled wobbegong
Orectolobus japonicus	Japanese wobbegong
Orectolobus maculatus	spotted wobbegong
Orectolobus ornatus	ornate wobbegong
Orectolobus wardi	Northern wobbegong
Sutorectus tentaculatus	cobbler wobbegong

Family: HEMISCYLLIDAE (longtailed carpetsharks, bamboo sharks)

Chiloscyllium arabicum	Arabian carpetshark
Chiloscyllium burmensis	Burmese bambooshark
Chiloscyllium griseum	gray bambooshark
Chiloscyllium hasselti	Indonesian bambooshark
Chiloscyllium indicum	slender bambooshark
Chiloscyllium plagiosum	whitespotted bambooshark
Chiloscyllium punctatum	brownbanded bambooshark
Hemiscyllium freycineti	Indonesian speckled carpetshark
Hemiscyllium hallstromi	Papuan epaulette shark
Hemiscyllium ocellatum	epaulette shark
Hemiscyllium strahani	hooded carpetshark
Hemiscyllium trispeculare	speckled carpetshark

Family: RHINIODONTIDAE (whale sharks, zebra sharks nurse sharks)

Ginglymostoma cirratum	nurse shark
Pseudoginglymostoma brevicaudatum	shorttail nurse shark
Nebrius ferrugineus	tawny nurse or giant sleepy shark
Stegostoma fasciatum	zebra shark
Rhiniodon typus	whale shark

Order: LAMNIFORMES (mackerel sharks)
Family: ODONTASPIDIDAE (sand tiger sharks)

Eugomphodus taurus	sand tiger, spotted raggedtooth, gray nurse shark
Eugomphodus tricuspidatus	Indian sand tiger
Odontaspis ferox	smalltooth sand tiger, bumpytail raggedtooth
Odontaspis noronhai	bigeye sand tiger

Family: MITSUKURINIDAE (goblin sharks)
Mitsukurina owstoni	goblin shark

Family: PSEUDOCARCHARIIDAE (crocodile sharks)
Pseudocarcharias kamoharai	crocodile shark

Family: MEGACHASMIDAE (megamouth sharks)
Megachasma pelagios	megamouth shark

Family: ALOPIIDAE (thresher sharks)

Alopias pelagicus	pelagic thresher
Alopias superciliosus	bigeye thresher
Alopias vulpinus	thresher shark

Family: CETORHINIDAE (basking sharks)
Cetorhinus maximus	basking shark

Family: LAMNIDAE (mackerel sharks)

Carcharodon carcharias	great white shark, maneater, white death
Isurus oxyrinchus	shortfin mako
Isurus paucus	longfin mako
Lamna ditropis	Pacific porbeagle, salmon shark
Lamna nasus	porbeagle, mackerel shark

Order: CARCHARHINIFORMES (ground sharks)
Family: SCYLIORHINIDAE (catsharks)

Apristurus abbreviatus	bignose catshark
Apristurus acanutus	flatnose catshark
Apristurus atlanticus	Atlantic ghost catshark
Apristurus brevicaudatus	
Apristurus brunneus	brown catshark
Apristurus canutus	hoary catshark
Apristurus federovi	Federov's catshark
Apristurus gibbosus	
Apristurus herklotsi	longfin catshark
Apristurus indicus	smallbelly catshark
Apristurus investigatoris	broadnose catshark
Apristurus japonicus	Japanese catshark
Apristurus kampae	longnose catshark
Apristurus laurussoni	Iceland catshark
Apristurus longianalis	
Apristurus longicaudatus	
Apristurus longicephalus	longhead catshark
Apristurus macrorhynchus	flathead catshark
Apristurus macrostomus	
Apristurus maderensis	Madeira catshark
Apristurus manis	ghost catshark
Apristurus microps	smalleye catshark
Apristurus micropterygeus	small dorsal catshark
Apristurus nasutus	largenose catshark
Apristurus parvipinnis	smallfin catshark
Apristurus pinguis	fat catshark
Apristurus platyrhynchus	spatulasnout catshark
Apristurus profundorum	deepwater catshark
Apristurus riveri	broadgill catshark
Apristurus saldanha	Saldanha catshark
Apristurus sibogae	pale catshark
Apristurus sinensis	South China catshark
Apristurus spongiceps	spongehead catshark
Apristurus stenseni	Panama ghost catshark
Apristurus verweyi	Borneo catshark
Apristurus xenolepis	oddscale catshark
Asymbolus analis	Australian spotted catshark
Asymbolus vincenti	Gulf catshark
Atelomycterus mackleayi	Australian marbled catshark
Atelomycterus marmoratus	coral catshark
Aulohalaelurus labiosus	blackspotted catshark
Cephaloscyllium fasciatum	reticulated swellshark
Cephaloscyllium isabellum	draughtsboard shark
Cephaloscyllium laticeps	Australian swellshark
Cephaloscyllium nascione	whitefinned swellshark
Cephaloscyllium silasi	Indian swellshark
Cephaloscyllium sufflans	balloon shark
Cephaloscyllium ventriosum	swellshark
Cephalurus cephalus	lollipop catshark
Galeus arae	roughtail catshark
Galeus boardmani	Australian sawtail catshark
Galeus eastmani	gecko catshark
Galeus longirostris	longnose sawtail catshark
Galeus melastomus	blackmouth catshark

Galeus murinus	mouse catshark
Galeus nipponensis	broadfin sawtail catshark
Galeus piperatus	peppered catshark
Galeus polli	African sawtail catshark
Galeus sauteri	blacktip sawtail catshark
Galeus schultzi	dwarf sawtail catshark
Halaelurus alcocki	Arabian catshark
Halaelurus boesemani	speckled catshark
Halaelurus buergeri	blackspotted catshark
Halaelurus canescens	dusky catshark
Halaelurus clevai	broadhead catshark
Halaelurus dawsoni	New Zealand catshark
Halaelurus hispidus	bristly catshark
Halaelurus immaculatus	spotless catshark
Halaelurus lineatus	lined catshark
Halaelurus lutarius	mud catshark
Halaelurus natalensis	tiger catshark
Halaelurus quagga	quagga catshark
Haploblepharus edwardsii	puffadder shyshark
Haploblepharus fuscus	brown shyshark
Haploblepharus pictus	dark shyshark
Holohalaelurus punctatus	African spotted catshark
Holohalaelurus regani	Izak catshark
Parmaturus campechiensis	Campeche catshark
Parmaturus macmillani	New Zealand filetail
Parmaturus melanobranchius	blackgill catshark
Parmaturus pilosus	salamander shark
Parmaturus xaniurus	filetail catshark
Pentanchus profundicolus	onefin catshark
Poroderma africanum	striped catshark, pyjama shark
Poroderma marleyi	barbeled catshark
Poroderma pantherinum	leopard catshark
Schroederichthys bivius	narrowmouth catshark
Schroederichthys chilensis	redspotted catshark
Schroederichthys maculatus	narrowtail catshark
Schroederichthys tenuis	slender catshark
Scyliorhinus besnardi	polkadot catshark
Scyliorhinus boa	boa catshark
Scyliorhinus canicula	smallspotted catshark
Scyliorhinus capensis	yellowspotted catshark
Scyliorhinus cervigoni	West African catshark
Scyliorhinus garmani	brownspotted catshark
Scyliorhinus haeckelii	freckled catshark
Scyliorhinus hesperius	whitesaddled catshark
Scyliorhinus meadi	blotched catshark
Scyliorhinus retifer	chain catshark
Scyliorhinus stellaris	nursehound
Scyliorhinus torazame	cloudy catshark
Scyliorhinus torrei	dwarf catshark

Family: PROSCYLLIIDAE (finback catsharks)

Ctenacis fehlmanni	harlequin catshark
Eridacnis barbouri	Cuban ribbontail catshark
Eridacnis radcliffei	pygmy ribbontail catshark
Eridacnis sinuans	African ribbontail catshark
Gollum attenuatus	slender smoothhound

Proscyllium habereri — graceful catshark

Family: PSEUDOTRIAKIDAE (false catsharks)

Pseudotriakis microdon — false catshark

Family: LEPTOCHARIIDAE (barbeled houndsharks)

Leptocharias smithii — barbeled houndshark

Family: TRIAKIDAE (houndsharks)

Furgaleus macki	whiskery shark
Galeorhinus galeus	school shark, tope shark, soupfin shark
Gogolia filewoodi	sailback houndshark
Hemitriakis japanica	Japanese topeshark
Hemitriakis leucoperiptera	whitefin topeshark
Hypogaleus hyugaensis	blacktip topeshark
Iago garricki	longnose houndshark
Iago omanensis	bigeye houndshark
Mustelus antarcticus	gummy shark
Mustelus asterias	starry smoothhound
Mustelus californicus	gray smoothhound
Mustelus canis	dusky smoothhound
Mustelus dorsalis	sharptooth or sharpnose smoothhound
Mustelus fasciatus	striped smoothhound
Mustelus griseus	spotless smoothhound
Mustelus henlei	brown smoothhound
Mustelus higmani	smalleye smoothhound
Mustelus lenticulatus	spotted estuary smoothhound, rig
Mustelus lunulatus	sicklefin smoothhound
Mustelus manazo	starspotted smoothhound
Mustelus mento	speckled smoothhound
Mustelus mosis	Arabian, hardnose or Moses smoothhound
Mustelus mustelus	smoothhound
Mustelus norrisi	narrowfin smoothhound or Florida dogfish
Mustelus palumbes	whitespot smoothhound
Mustelus punctulatus	blackspot smoothhound
Mustelus schmitti	narrownose smoothhound
Mustelus whitneyi	humpback smoothhound
Scylliogaleus quecketti	flapnose houndshark
Triakis acutipinna	sharpfin houndshark
Triakis maculata	spotted houndshark
Triakis megalopterus	sharptooth houndshark or spotted gully shark
Triakis scyllium	banded houndshark
Triakis semifasciata	leopard shark

Family: HEMIGALEIDAE (weasel sharks)

Chaenogaleus macrostoma	hooktooth shark
Hemigaleus microstoma	sicklefin weasel shark
Hemipristis elongatus	snaggletooth shark
Paragaleus leucolomatus	whitetip weasel shark
Paragaleus pectoralis	Atlantic weasel shark
Paragaleus tengi	straighttooth weasel shark

Family: CARCHARHINIDAE (requiem sharks)

Carcharhinus acronotus	blacknose shark
Carcharhinus albimarginatus	silvertip shark
Carcharhinus altimus	bignose shark
Carcharhinus amblyrhynchoides	graceful shark
Carcharhinus amblyrhynchos	gray reef shark
Carcharhinus amboinensis	pigeye or Java shark
Carcharhinus borneensis	Borneo shark
Carcharhinus brachyurus	copper shark or bronze whaler
Carcharhinus brevipinna	spinner shark
Carcharhinus cautus	nervous shark
Carcharhinus dussumieri	whitecheek shark
Carcharhinus falciformis	silky shark
Carcharhinus fitzroyensis	creek whaler
Carcharhinus galapagensis	Galapagos shark
Carcharhinus hemiodon	Pondicherry shark
Carcharhinus isodon	finetooth shark
Carcharhinus leucas	bull, Nicaragua or Zambesi shark
Carcharhinus limbatus	blacktip shark
Carcharhinus longimanus	oceanic whitetip shark
Carcharhinus macloti	hardnose shark
Carcharhinus melanopterus	blacktip reef shark
Carcharhinus obscurus	dusky shark
Carcharhinus perezi	Caribbean reef shark
Carcharhinus plumbeus	sandbar shark
Carcharhinus porosus	smalltail shark
Carcharhinus sealei	blackspot shark
Carcharhinus signatus	night shark
Carcharhinus sorrah	spottail shark
Carcharhinus wheeleri	blacktail reef shark
Galeocerdo cuvier	tiger shark
Glyphis gangeticus	Ganges shark
Glyphis glyphis	speartooth shark
Isogomphodon oxyrhynchus	daggernose shark
Lamiopsis temmincki	broadfin shark
Loxodon macrorhinus	sliteye shark
Nasolamia velox	whitenose shark
Negaprion acutidens	sharptooth lemon shark
Negaprion brevirostris	lemon shark
Prionace glauca	blue shark, blue whaler
Rhizoprionodon acutus	milk shark
Rhizoprionodon lalandii	Brazilian sharpnose shark
Rhizoprionodon longurio	Pacific sharpnose shark
Rhizoprionodon oligolinx	gray sharpnose shark
Rhizoprionodon porosus	Caribbean sharpnose shark
Rhizoprionodon taylori	Australian sharpnose shark
Rhizoprionodon terraenovae	Atlantic sharpnose shark
Scoliodon laticaudus	spadenose shark
Triaenodon obesus	whitetip reef shark

Family: SPHYRNIDAE (hammerhead sharks)

Eusphyra blochii	winghead shark
Sphyrna corona	mallethead shark
Sphyrna lewini	scalloped hammerhead
Sphyrna media	scoophead shark
Sphyrna mokarran	great hammerhead
Sphyrna tiburo	shovelhead shark or bonnethead shark
Sphyrna tudes	smalleye hammerhead
Sphyrna zygaena	smooth hammerhead, balance fish